OPERATION: OFFICE SLEUTH

GIVE ZERO F*CKS AT WORK

FOR AN AMAZINGLY PRODUCTIVE AND SATISFYING WORK-LIFE BALANCE

GERARD HENRY

Operation: Office Sleuth

Copyright © 2019 by Gerard Henry

Manufactured in the United States of America

All rights reserved. No part of this book may be reproduced in any form or by any electronic or mechanical means including information storage and retrieval systems without permission in writing from the publisher, except for a reviewer, who may quote brief passages in a review.

First Edition, 2019

ISBN: 9781673312164

Firefalls Publishing, LLC

info@firefallspublishing.com

www.Firefallspublishing.com

www.officesleuth.com

TABLE OF CONTENTS

PREFACE I

INTRODUCTION VII

CHAPTER 1 - BUSY WORK 1

CHAPTER 2 - THE BIG PROJECT 7

CHAPTER 3 - MANAGING YOUR DAY-TO-DAY 19

CHAPTER 4 - THE OVER-ACHIEVING BOSS 29

CHAPTER 5 - CHOOSE YOUR BATTLES... WISELY 37

CHAPTER 6 - THE AFTER-VACATION SYNDROME 49

CHAPTER 7 - WHAT IS A MICRO-MANAGER 63

CHAPTER 8 – MANAGERS VS LEADERS 103

CHAPTER 9 – ACING THE SELF REVIEW 113

CHAPTER 10 – THE SIT DOWN 123

CHAPTER 11 – GOALS, YOUR FUTURE REALIZED NOW 143

CHAPTER 12 - FREEDOM - OUR END GOAL 165

CHAPTER 13- CONCLUSION 177

APPENDIX I 187

APPENDIX II 203

APPENDIX III 207

PREFACE

It was the early 90's. I was a freshman in college. I went to a college about 4 hours away from my parent's house, so I stayed in the dorm at the college, I "went away" to college as we called it. After hanging out at several parties, I started to click with a particular fraternity. I started hanging out with them outside of parties. Since I was living away from home and didn't have too many friends at school, I started thinking about joining this fraternity, pledging it's called. Growing up, I never really thought about fraternities. I didn't leave home for college, dying to join a frat. But things happen, and the more time I spent time with my new friends, the more interested I became in pledging the fraternity.

After a little while, I met up with other pledge candidates, and we also started hanging out regularly. So, when it came time to start the pledge process, there were six people in our little clique. Our tight-knit group became the pledge class - The Epsilon Elite.

During the pledge process, we would get calls in the middle of the night to meet up places and do things, whether it was a scavenger hunt or just sitting on a wall all night, or some other activity that would cause sleep deprivation. Looking back, I think that pledging was an enjoyable time. It allowed the pledge class to bond with each other. Thankfully there was no real hazing in my fraternity Every so often I hear horror stories about an unfortunate person who got hurt or even died from the pledging process, luckily, we didn't have to deal with that.

The whole time I pledged this fraternity (about eight weeks if I recall correctly) I was always the nervous one. Instead of getting a pledge task and just having fun with it, I always stressed about making sure we completed the activity. What would happen if we didn't? (Basically, nothing would happen, but I was the paranoid, nervous guy in the pledge class.) This made it harder for the rest of the pledge class because I caused this unnecessary stress.

My roommate in the college dorm got used to the calls in the middle of the night. And this was way before cell phones, so those "calls" were more like someone knocking on the dorm room door at 2 a.m. He was a good sport about it, but my decision to pledge, coupled with my paranoia about not screwing anything up, probably made me a bit of an unbearable roommate at the time. If you are reading this, Crosby, I apologize.

The last week of pledging is something referred to as Hell Week. This is the week right before pledging ends, and it forces the pledge class into ever-increasing, tougher projects and situations. Some are timed, some cause sleep deprivation, some are awkward - dealing with neighboring sororities for specific items (I'll leave it at that).

Hell Week takes the pledge process and ramps up the intensity over a week-long period. I am sure my pledge class was thrilled about going through Hell Week with me in the pledge class. Having an anxious person in your pledge class during the normal pledging process is bad enough, during Hell Week that nervousness would amp up exponentially. Or at least that's what everybody thought.

Something happened inside of my brain right at the beginning of Hell Week. During one of the first of our ever-increasing tasks, I thought and then vocalized the fact that I didn't give a f*ck! I stopped caring about anything. I didn't care if we finished on time, I didn't care if we finished at all. It was as if a weight was lifted off my shoulders, blinders taken off my eyes, allowing me to see clearly. It was a time that everyone thought would be a nightmare (mainly because of me) but probably became the best week of my college life. We had so much fun that week because we all adopted the I don't give a F*ck mantra.

Besides finishing up the worst week of pledging relatively stress-free, it also allowed the entire pledge class's bond to become even stronger. We were laughing at all the stupid things we had to do rather than get stressed out. The rest of the pledge class and I got along great that week, probably for the first time since we started pledging. By giving zero F*cks we were able to get everything done with minimal stress. We worked better as a team, and all became members of the fraternity that week. We'd go on to have a fantastic bond that lasts even today.

I don't know what would have happened if I didn't look at the situation for what it was, a game. Instead of stressing over every phone call, we just bonded and had fun. Guess what, everything that needed to get done got done. All the stress in the world wasn't helping us complete tasks timelier or made us look better to the fraternity (or anyone else in the college that saw us) by not having stress in our lives allowed us to get more things done quicker and more accurately.

Besides being in the fraternity and accomplishing that goal, I realized that this stress-free, give zero F*cks lifestyle probably works other places as well. So, throughout my personal and professional life, I always try and work the zero F*ck lifestyle into every situation. Whenever I feel angry or anxious, I think, "I will probably laugh about this someday," so why not make someday today? It's like one time I went to the UPS store to ship two packages to two separate addresses. They were both relatively high dollar items that couldn't be replaced, so when I found out the people at the UPS store shipped each package to the wrong person, my blood pressure rose a bit. These were eBay auctions, so they weren't people I knew (like a family member) that I could call and have them send back the package.

Once the initial phase of the stress subsided, I said to myself I will laugh about this one day, but right now I cannot give a F*ck, I can only fix this. I went to the UPS store and explained the situation. Luckily, they were able to recall both packages (oh did

I mention that the contents were expensive old bottles of scotch, so I didn't even know if I was allowed to ship them in the first place). So now I'm having two separate bottles of scotch returned to the UPS store (and this may not even be allowed, I'm not sure). I have to make sure to get there when these packages arrive and make sure the UPS Store people do not open the boxes. I need to explain to the two buyers that there was a mix-up, and now their packages will be delayed.

Guess what, everything went according to plan. The UPS store received the packages and then shipped them to the right addresses. I think the whole store knew about this since I called and went down to the store multiple times to correct this. Both buyers received their packages, albeit it took a little longer than expected, but I was in constant contact with them, providing tracking numbers and explaining everything.

Instead of freaking out and not doing what I needed to do, I gave zero F*cks, remained stress-free, took care of the packages, and now I have a story I can laugh about. This is how I live my life, and it works wonders. My blood pressure is nice and low (or at least normal.) I think you can work this lifestyle in every area of your life. Not only to help relieve everyday stresses but to work smarter, more efficient. Working smarter, coupled with a stress-free lifestyle, will help you to accomplish more by doing less. People often ask me, "I see how you can do this in your personal life because you have total control, but what about at work. I have to play by the company rules. Plus, they are paying me to do a job, so shouldn't I give a F*ck at work?" The simple answer is yes, and no, I always say you should care about your job, but do that job on your terms (and by your terms means giving zero F*cks.) I know this sounds completely counter-intuitive, but after reading this life manual (or book as my publisher likes to call it), you will do less work while remaining stress-free and become much more productive in the process. I can't guarantee this book will help you find your way into the corner office (if that is what you desire), but this will give you the work-life balance you crave.

Let's get started.

INTRODUCTION

Can you really give zero F*cks at work? Or maybe you should be asking, should I not really care about my job or career or whatever you call the thing you do that brings in a paycheck every week. Now I'm talking about doing work for someone who isn't either you or a close relative. I'm talking about working for someone who has a current need that you can fill, and if that need goes away tomorrow, then there is a good chance that you'll be exiting the building right alongside that need.

I'll also mention that you have to figure out exactly how marketable you are in the workplace. If you spent six months finding your current job and you may be spending another six months finding another job if you were let go, you may want to think twice about taking all my advice. I still think you will become a much more relaxed and productive member of your team after reading this book. But ultimately, don't do anything that you think you'll regret.

Let me tell you the story of how this whole philosophy came about. First off, I never really thought I made "TOO MUCH" money. What I mean is I could always find another job at another company for pretty much the same money relatively easy. (I work in an office in the accounting / finance field.) So, I have to say that I was never really worried about losing my job. I believe I bring a lot of value to my company and every company I've ever worked, and to this day I've never been fired from a job. Oh, except one time when I was 14 and working in a bakery. I'd go there every day after school and wash dishes, pots, pans, and utensils. I came across what looked like a wooden spoon except it didn't have the spoon part; it was just a stick. So, I threw it out. Low and behold, it wasn't just a stick, and somehow the guy who owned the bakery found this wooden dowel in the garbage. The next time I came to work, he showed up, he stopped by the bakery in the afternoon (something he never did) confronted me about the stick and fired my ass. Lesson learned; one man's stick is another man's treasure.

So, what drove me to the point of not giving a F*ck whether or not I was fired or promoted?

Three times is my answer.

The funny thing is that working in accounting, or at least in higher-level accounting positions, I have access to all of the payroll records of the companies I've worked. So, I see what people make, and I know how much work they actually do each day. Mainly, I look at my boss and compare myself to him. So, my whole philosophy started when I watched my boss take all of the work I did and meet with the board of directors and take credit for everything. He never let me get too close to the top management team. Now you might say that he was buffering me from them. At some companies, you may be correct. But you have to believe me when I tell you that he ran 95% of every accounting or finance-related decision by me. My boss would come into my office and ask me the most basic accounting questions.

On the one hand, I'm glad he did because then I could be sure that the work would be done correctly. But on the other hand, knowing how much money he makes and then comparing it to how much money I am paid, the math didn't make sense. Factoring in salary and bonus, he makes about three times the amount of money I make, and yet he depends on me to implement about 95% of the procedures in our department, while he takes all of the credit. You don't have to be a C.P.A. to see that the math doesn't make sense.

Now luckily for me, my boss is clueless about a lot of things, mainly technological things. So, something that would take him all day to prepare, I could probably put together in an hour or two. So, this leaves me with a lot of wiggle room.

Let me tell you the story of my big promotion and what a bullshit thing that turned into. In order to let someone, go in my company, who was a good employee but not really needed, I offered to take over two departments that he managed. These departments were a finance function, so it just made sense that I merge them into the finance group. After selling this idea to the owner, the Chief Operation Officer, and of course, the Chief Financial Officer, they let this guy go, saving the company a high

6-figure salary. Now unfortunately for me, all of this happened before I finalized any deal about my promotion (I am managing two additional departments, and I just saved the company about $200k, so I didn't think anyone would play games with me, but boy was I wrong.)

Initially, my boss said he was going to talk about my compensation arraignment with the owner and the executive team. This conversation took place before firing the other guy. I guess this was my fault because as soon as they fired him and introduced me as the new department head of the new group, my boss's tune changed. It went from I'll talk with them about your compensation to why don't you work with the two groups for a while and let's show them that your plan is working. So I just saved the company $200k, I've doubled my workload, and they want to see if this plan is working? When I received that email, yes, for anything that is potentially confrontational my boss emails me, I was livid. Well, according to my boss, my official review was coming up in about 3-4 months, and that would be the perfect amount of time to show everyone the progress I could make. I took on all of the responsibility and did get the title, but none of the compensation. But I'm a team player, and I'm sure my raise in 3 months would be HELLA BIG (at least that is what I thought.)

To make a long story short, I worked for the three months with the other departments, made significant improvements, and helped create a more synergistic work environment between all the departments in finance. Now, without getting into specifics, I made a salary comparison for my new position, and I expected about a $30k raise in salary and an adjustment to my bonus. The way I saw it, I just saved the company $200k and worked for three months completely underpaid, so I didn't think this was unreasonable. So, I go into my review prepared with my research from multiple sources showing salary ranges of my new position at companies similar in size and location. He says he needs a number to go back to the executive team with, and I give him the lowest level in every range (Which is the amount I mentioned before, the $30k.) He goes back, and then a few days later, I get an email (yep, not even a face to face conversation) saying he is giving me $5k increase, and he'll increase my bonus % a bit. He also adds that he "thinks this is very good." (Yes, good for him and the company but certainly not for me.) As I'm sure you can imagine, I hit the F*cking roof when I read that email, so I went back into his office to speak to him. Let me ask you if you ever worked for one of these types, any time I have a face-to-face meeting about my compensation he always starts by saying "You know if it were up to me, I'd pay you a million dollars." Well, the one thing I do know is that you are the one making this bullshit decision, but you'd love for me to be stupid enough to believe you that it wasn't your decision at all. After a bit of back and forth, I only got another; "We still have to see how this works", but I knew that once I accepted the offer, I wasn't getting any more money. He thought that he screwed me. Twice the work for basically the same pay. An employer's dream.

I'm sure at this point you must be asking yourself, "Why don't you just quit and find another job?" Well, believe me, that thought crossed my mind, probably every minute for the next month and now only every 10 minutes. But I had it pretty good; otherwise, the job was a quick commute for me, and my team was excellent. So instead of quitting, I made up my mind to give zero F*cks and see how long I can remain employed. As of this writing, I'm on about two and a half years, so what you'll learn in this book really works.

So, without further ado, let me show you exactly how I committed to work on the day I decided to give zero F*cks. The funny thing is that my stress has completely disappeared, I've become much more productive, and my quality of life has drastically improved.

CHAPTER 1 - BUSY WORK

Did you ever have one of those days? You know the type; you are staring at the clock with absolutely nothing to do. Every assignment and responsibility on your plate has been completed. You are left, scrambling, looking high and low for anything to do! It's not like your boss will walk by any minute and ask you what you are working on right now?

Funny story, I used to work for a C.P.A. firm where all of the staff accountants sat in cubicles in the middle of the office. Around the perimeter of the building were offices. Did you ever get that feeling that someone was staring at you, or you felt like you were being watched? At this company, I always seemed to feel that way. One time, when my spider-senses started to tingle, I looked over my right shoulder; there was this partner that I worked for, with his head almost on my shoulder, staring at my computer. Once I noticed him, he'd go, "What are you working on?" Creepy...

But back to my original question, were you ever at work and wished you suddenly remembered some big project that you had to complete. Not because you felt like doing more work for the company, but because you literally finished everything on your agenda for the day. This is the point where people tend to get in trouble, they start playing with their phones, or become a regular social butterfly and stop by everyone's office/cubicle to see what's up.

Now any manager (who actually gives a F*ck) will tell you at this point that you should ask for something to do, but I found a few reasons why this isn't always the best idea. First of all, if you are asking for more work and you still have half the day to go, and this happens regularly, then management will have to assess whether or not they have too many people in the department. So either you find yourself in H.R. having "the talk," thanks, but we don't have the amount of work we initially thought when we hired you. Sorry? Or maybe management believes you are a Rockstar, fires someone else, and then "rewards" you by giving you all of their work. Trust me, it happens.

So, my entire point of this chapter is going to try and answer one of the most fundamental questions that I always asked myself as an employee, I'm sure at one point you've asked yourself (Or at least thought about). "Do I have a specific set of tasks that I am being paid to perform in a day, or do I just keep performing tasks until the clock strikes 5 o'clock?"

Let's think about the answer from an employer's perspective. The idea of telling someone "Here is your work assignment for the day" then let them manage the workflow sounds like a much better idea than the alternative. But you know the company likes the idea of getting eight hours of work out of an employee and no matter how much work they finish just keep giving them more and more. This sounds really good around the board room, but let's look at this in practice.

Say you perform five projects in one day, you were initially assigned three, but then after completing the three, you asked what you should be working on, so along came project four, then five. The first thing this employee will notice is how many projects everyone else is performing. If the rest of the department only gets the original three projects completed each day, then you can bet that our Rockstar employee will start to slow down over time. They won't try for the fifth project, and eventually, they will begin skipping the fourth project. I firmly believe in Parkinson's Law - Work expands to fill the time available.

So, you start taking the full day to complete the three original projects. This leads back to my original question. Are you supposed to finish a set amount of work in a day or keep tackling new work until the end of the day? I know that employers will argue that they are paying you for the full day, regardless of how many projects you finish. Unfortunately for employers, the employees also realize this, so they can start to control how slow they work. I've thought about this for years, wouldn't it be better to give people a certain amount of work in a day and let them manage getting it done? If the Rockstar finishes in four hours, then they leave work after four hours. If slow-poke Sam takes ten hours to complete the same tasks, then Sam has to work ten hours. What a concept?

Now this will never fly with modern corporate employers, so people spend half the day "finding" things to do. Ever notice that anytime an employer tells an employee that they can go home after they finish a particular task, that task will be done almost instantaneously. Either the employee already had the job done, or they speed up to normal, but to everyone else, they appear to have doubled their "normal speed."

This is where the saying don't get mad, get even comes in to play. Especially if your direct manager is clueless, and you can work circles around him (or her) or when the boss lies (or forgets) about things (mainly compensation-related things). Isn't it funny? My boss remembers every mistake I made the entire F*ckin' year, but conveniently forgets the conversation about the bonus or pay increase that we had last week? Now my current gig is pretty good, I work close to home, I get paid reasonably well, and my boss is clueless, so I don't want to give this up. But whenever my boss conveniently forgets a promise he made or something like that, and I get the urge to quit (and I've come close on several occasions), instead of quitting on the spot, I always take a few deep breaths and say to myself, "Take the weekend to make up your mind", so I take a full weekend and weigh the pros and cons.

Here's how the conversation in my head goes (and no, I'm not a psycho, I swear), I make x dollars for doing about 4 hours of work in a day (and believe me, I get all of my work done, you can't slack and not get your work done.) But is it slacking? My boss does about one-quarter of the work I can do, he asks my opinion about pretty much everything and gets paid about triple what I make. So is it slacking? If the boss in my example above can only complete two projects, sometimes three, in the allotted time. And he earns three times what I make. Am I slacking for finishing only three or four projects a day? It helps if you are the "right-hand man" (or women) you tend to have more leeway, but the question remains, am I a slacker for working AS FAST as my boss? Ideally, I'd like to be able to leave my office once my work for the day is finished or ultimately work from home. This way, I can do other things that are important (more on this later.)

OK, I'm going to leave you in this chapter to ponder these questions:

"Am I a slacker?" and, more importantly, "Do I have a specific set of tasks that I am being paid to perform in a day, or do I just keep performing tasks until the clock strikes five o'clock?"

In the next chapter, we'll touch on the all-important question of how do I look busy if I'm trapped in my office/cubicle for eight hours and how to field the insidious email "Send me what's on your to-do list?"

CHAPTER 2 - THE BIG PROJECT

So, after having a frustrating run-in with my boss. Whether he's taking credit for my work or coming down with a case of selective amnesia when it comes to my raise and bonus. I'm left with two choices: A. Quit or B. look busy while doing the absolute minimum amount of work I can do without tipping him off. After taking the weekend to consider my options, I come to my senses and go with option B - Look busy while doing next to nothing.

I want to start by saying I'm not a lazy person by nature. I've been working since the seventh grade with my own paper route. One route turned into four or five paper routes (that I absorbed into my own as the surrounding routes became available). I worked on Saturdays for $10 handing out the Sunday comics to all of the other paper delivery people. Come to think of it, before having my own paper route, I used to help my friend with his paper route for a few bucks a week. I've always hustled, raking leaves, mowing lawns, even babysitting. I'm not advocating laziness. I'm just thinking about my job, the work I do, how much my manager depends on me, and the times I was passed over for a promotion. When I say passed over, I mean overall career advancement. Anything from giving me a crappy raise, usurping me in one of my roles because he had the hots for one of my employees, always eavesdropping then popping into my office and start asking questions about a personal conversation... The list goes on.

My main gripe is that he makes a hell of a lot more money than me; meanwhile, I make about 90% of the decisions and do the majority of the work. (Does this sound familiar?) I work much more efficiently, so I am much faster, and that is a big part of the problem. Like I mentioned in the last chapter, I can perform a task three to four times faster than he can. Partly because of technology (he works with a very manual process), partly because he doesn't seem to understand things half the time (more on this later). The worst is when we agree on a process that would be beneficial to the department. Then he goes to a meeting without me and ends up caving in and changing the entire process when someone else makes a request. It's probably the most frustrating thing of all.

By him caving into other group's demands, it makes my department's job that much tougher. Since he doesn't actually do the work, he doesn't actually know the steps involved in the process. He has no idea how much extra work he is creating for my group and me. As frustrating as this is, and it's really f*cking frustrating, the extra work actually has a silver lining. That is a good thing (Especially when my boss just unnecessarily agreed to a process twice as complex as it had to be.) The first thing we need to do is try to figure out how long this task would take him to complete (even though he doesn't even understand what to do) and then get down to the business at hand, looking busy.

STEP ONE - THE MULTIPLE

I'm a firm believer in the multiple. The multiple is a phrase I've coined for the ratio between the time it would take my boss to complete a task versus how long I can complete the job. I always round up or down to be as conservative as possible. This will only benefit me in the long run. Suppose I am given a task that would take the boss a full day to finish, so that would be eight hours. Now to be conservative, I'll factor in an hour for phones and an hour for chit-chat, internet… whatever. I'll put his REAL time in at six hours. Let's say that using a more automated approach, I think I can complete this job between an hour to an hour and a half, again to be conservative. I'll round my time UP to two hours. This gives me a multiple of three (His six hours divided by my two hours.)

What exactly does a multiple of three mean?

It means, conservatively, however long it took me actually to complete the task, I can spend an additional 2x worth of time doing something for me. Now, why 2x? Since the first third of the multiple was, you actually completing the job and you are left with double (2x) the amount of time the task took you to complete for "personal time".

So assuming my example above, you finish that job in the two hours, your boss thinks it should take around six hours (especially after you complain and tell him how much extra time his caving in has caused your department), so that gives you an additional four hours of what I call... Me time

STEP TWO - FIGURE OUT IN ADVANCE WHAT TO DO WITH YOUR *PERSONAL TIME*

Personal time could be anything, but I hate to waste it on things like aimlessly surfing the web, checking Facebook, or watching YouTube videos. Unless the web surfing or YouTube watching was for a specific purpose, like researching which car you are going to buy, or saving time researching how to do something, so you don't spend half your night having to research it. That would be perfectly acceptable. If you think that your boss doesn't do all of the things you are thinking about doing, then either you have a nutty boss (which is the perfect reason to start updating the resume), or you don't know what is going on when he/she closes their door.

Other things I do during, what I call personal time:

- Updating a website
- Writing a blog post
- Trade stock (Use your phone so IT can't see your info)
- Actively search for a new position (If you have one of those nutty bosses)
- Write a book, either whole chapter or at least jot down your ideas in the form of an outline
- Learn how to do something that you'll otherwise have to research at home (on your REAL time off)

- Paying bills (Use your phone if you think IT can see your web activity)
- Research purchases, like cars, homes, TV's
- Find a doctor or a specialist
- Get your holiday shopping done (Via Amazon)
- Learn something new, watch videos, read webpages or just read a book in PDF format on your computer

You get the idea. This list can be endless. I use this time to accomplish something. Let's be honest, you could get fired for reading a book or writing a blog post, so if I'm taking that kind of risk, I want to make sure I do something during work hours that will save me time after hours when I'm home with my family.

Funny story, I worked with this one guy who somehow conditioned his body to have to go to the bathroom at work every day. He'd always say something like, "They're paying me to take a shit." Which is accurate and not far off from what I am recommending. I just proactively kick it up a notch.

STEP THREE - TIMING

Once you know how long it takes to complete a task, and you're reasonably comfortable that it's accurate. (e.g., if you've already done the job and are reasonably sure you can get it done in an hour and a half. With a multiple of three (1.5 hours x 3 = 4.5 hours), that gives you three hours of personal time (4.5 hours - 1.5 hours it actually takes to complete the task)). One key in doing this is to allow the extra (multiple) of time right from the beginning. If your boss asks how long it will take, just give him an estimate of half a day or so. You don't want to finish the job in two hours the first time and then start letting project drag to three or four hours in subsequent months, you're better off starting at four hours and then you can pull it back to three if you really want to look like the office Super Hero (especially if you're trying to get promoted or a good raise).

So how is the best way to handle the allotted personal time?

This is entirely up to you. Sometimes I like just to get the task done. I go straight through it without stopping, and about 90 minutes later, I have a completed project that can be sent off. I'm left with about three hours for my own time. Again, if you feel weird or bad, you don't have to take a full three hours. Maybe just take an extra hour. Try it out and see if it works for you. I still look at it this way; if my boss did the task, it would take him about six hours, so unless he is really monitoring what I'm doing, it will seem perfectly reasonable to him that I took only four hours (give or take a half-hour.)

Secondly, as I mentioned earlier, he caved to another department without even asking me. I already explained why the new way is going to take forever. I let him know that it's his fault. I can't reprimand my direct manager or supervisor, but I can let them know how much extra time it's costing the department and me. Just make sure that you pad that time sufficiently.

Lastly, it all goes back to how many projects my manager is tasking me to perform in a day and what it's worth to him/her. If I get paid $200 a day, and I'm given one task to accomplish that day, then that task is worth $200 to my manager. So, in this example, if I finish this task and immediately ask for something else, I will probably be given something that my manager has been procrastinating on doing. Now I finished my job for the day, so my day just freed up. And now, I have the privilege of doing it. (Not to mention that my boss makes like three times what I make, so taking work from him so he can have more "personal time" doesn't make a lot of business sense to me. It definitely does to the company, but not to me.)

The other thing about timing and this is true even if you would never implement any of the ideas in this book, you should ALWAYS give yourself ample cushion to get a task completed. Suppose you get the job done in 90 minutes, and you know you can always get the job done in 90 minutes, always give yourself a cushion. Always tell them it will take at least two or two and hour hours. So you're not left with an abundance of time, but you are giving you some cushion. Here's why.

This is a true story, and it is relevant to this idea of giving yourself some cushion. When I was going to college, I worked overnight at a very large package delivery company. I was promoted to supervisor and supervised about 40 people, most of them loaded the package delivery trucks and the others would take packages coming from a conveyor belt and sort them into different color bins for the guys loading trucks (Each truck was loaded from a different color bin - this truck might use the top blue bin or middle yellow, you get the idea.) The company had certain minimums it required the people to achieve, a metric they called pieces per hour. Everyone was measured by the number of pieces per hour that they either sorted from the conveyor belts or loaded on to the trucks (Whichever job you did.)

Now to make sure nobody was goofing off, they would have me climb up on a conveyor belt 40 feet off the ground (Thankfully, it wasn't actually moving at the time) and watch what the guys on the sort were doing. I'd wait and count and see why certain people did and didn't make the pieces per hour quota. This was pretty sneaky. I mention this because your company is always watching in some form or another. The other thing I did was work directly with the guys loading the trucks. Say the required pieces per hour were 200 and a particular guy was only loading 185, the company would have me work with him, show him how to sort the packages and make fewer trips into the truck, eventually getting his piece count to the required 200 pieces per hour.

Now here's where it gets interesting, suppose for 15 minutes he follows everything I said and with me watching (and counting) he does 50 pieces. So, I can extrapolate that 50 pieces in 15 minutes equal 200 in an hour. So, technically, he can load 200 pieces per hour. So according to the company, he did it for those 15 minutes, so now he is expected (and required) to load 200 pieces per hour. Before, he had a little cushion, but by doing the full 200 pieces per hour for only 15 minutes proves that he could, so now they expect it.

Here is my point, if you never gave yourself any cushion and immediately send the finished work over to your manager as soon as it was completed, then he/she will always expect that you finish that job in 90 minutes. And then if it does take you two hours to do it one time, you'll have to explain why it took you an extra half an hour. So please trust me when I say always give yourself a little cushion.

STEP FOUR - HOW TO HANDLE THE INQUISITION

Inevitably, you will run into what I like to call The Inquisition. This is when you will get caught with a litany of questions about what is the ETA? Did you send the report to so-and-so? Can you start on a new project?

Let's talk about how to answer these questions. First off, you never want to look up at your boss when he/she goes "What is the ETA?" and say "Oh, here is the completed project, I'm emailing you now." You don't want him/her to think you've been sitting on the work (even though you probably have been. And if you've been listening to anything, I've said so far, then you definitely have been spacing out the distribution of projects.) But on the flipside, you don't want to have nothing to show the boss. This is why I like to rifle through the work then take a little breather afterward. You don't have to finish the task at hand completely, but you should be pretty close to done if a reasonable amount of time has gone by.

(For example, you are working on a project you can do in an hour, but you usually take two hours before you send it back to the boss. By the first hour, you should have a fair amount of the job done. Don't wait until the second hour to start the job. You will be totally screwed during an inquisition. Trust me.)

Usually, when I'm asked about the ETA of a project, even though it might be finished, I still give myself a little cushion. You can accomplish this in a few ways. You can just say that you need about 20 minutes to complete the project. I find 20 minutes is a good amount of cushion. If it's an urgent project, you can send it a little quicker (10-15 minutes) and look good in your boss's eyes, or just send it at the 20-minute mark. I also use 20 minutes because I can get a lot done in 20 minutes. I can read up on a topic I'm researching, I can watch a 30 minute YouTube video (at 1.5x speed), I can write a good amount of a blog post.. etc.

The other way I handle questions based on the ETA of a project is I say I'm double-checking the report. I make a habit of always double-checking my work anyway, so the project would have already been double-checked (So it's no lie, for anyone who has a hard time stretching the truth.) Let's be honest, depending on the project, it could be something that will go straight to the president and board directors, so in that case, I'd probably use the last 20 minutes and triple-check my work. You have to evaluate what you are working on and make that determination.

The "I'm just double-checking" need for additional time is probably the best reason to give a manager that likes to micro-manage. I find micro-managers will not only ask you, but they will want to see your work. Plus, if your manager is anything like some of the micro-managing managers I've worked with, they want to sit down and look over your work, even though they don't 100% understand what or how you compiled the project. So they will waste a ton of time asking you to explain where every number came from, and you end up adding an additional hour to the project. This usually isn't so bad if I email the report directly to the manager. Usually, a few phone calls but not an all-day sit-down session to go over everything in the report (Beware of the calendar invite to review in his/her office… usually turns in to a regular all-day grilling session.)

So if the project has been completed, it becomes a tougher sell to say you need 20 minutes to complete. I'm double-checking my work is code for I am finished but need some more time before I send it to you. Another massive benefit about sending it over to the boss later rather than sooner is if this project is time-sensitive, meaning your boss needs to send it out to other people in the company (or outside of the company) then sending it to them closer to the deadline leaves much less time for them to sit with you and go over every single number. Your work better be right because if there are mistakes, it will reflect poorly on your boss, and he won't trust you the next time (Meaning, an extra-long meeting to tick and tie out every number on the report is almost guaranteed.) But if your work is correct and he/she doesn't have a lot of time between you finishing and having to send it, then no long-ass meetings. The key is to get your boss's trust (More on this later.)

In this chapter, we took a look at how to manage larger one-off and ad-hoc projects:

1. Calculate the multiple

2. Figure out what to do with your *Personal Time*

3. How to time a project

4. How to answer the inevitable litany of questions

In the next chapter, we will discuss how you manage your day-to-day job functions. This is the meat and potatoes of your workday, week, month. I know it sounds like I am encouraging you to slack all day, but believe me, managing all of your day-to-day activities will make you a much more productive employee. (And managing your day-to-day the way I will show you will also make you a much less stressed employee.)

CHAPTER 3 - MANAGING YOUR DAY-TO-DAY

Let's quickly recap. We are getting paid to do work. If you made me an offer to rake and bag leaves for $100, then all I would be required to do to earn that $100 would be to rake and bag the leaves. If halfway through the job, you smashed a large glass table on your front lawn and wanted help cleaning up the glass, it wouldn't be included in the $100 price, right? Unless this was a relative or an elderly neighbor that you would help regardless of payment, you must remember that you're not doing this work for free. It's a job. Your time has value, and we've established that value when we agreed on a price to rake the leaves for $100. If the raking takes five hours, then you've priced your time at $20/hour. You can use this as a benchmark to price out cleaning up the glass, but make sure you factor in the danger of picking up the glass. Maybe you need special gloves, so you don't cut up your hands, so that's an extra cost. You estimate that the actual work of cleaning the glass will take you an hour, but due to the additional cost of the gloves we had to buy and factoring the risk of cutting your hands, we price the job at $50.

There are a couple of things to think about in the above example. First of all, the extra work of cleaning up the glass was not part of the original price. Since you are working to earn money, you should absolutely charge for that work (in addition to doing the leaf raking job). Think of this glass cleaning job as an amendment to the first job. Also, we learned that this job included extra responsibility (risk). So we charged more for the work (think about the idea of working out of title or out of scope, doing a manager's job when you are not in management, and you are not being paid the same as a manager). Lastly, we originally priced our time at $20/hour, but due to the risk of the glass clean-up, we were able to increase our overall hourly rate to $30/ hour ($100 +$50 = $150/6 total hours = $30/hour).

Now the correlation I want you to make is that the homeowner (The boss) would have been happy to just include the glass clean-up in the original $100. And even after you made the argument that the clean-up will take an extra hour of your time (the time you could be spending making more money at another job or having an extra hour to do whatever you want, Personal Time). So the homeowner (boss) probably expects to give you another $20 to do the hours' worth of cleaning. So you have to explain the additional risk (Potential cuts and the extra cost for gloves), and finally, he agrees to pay you the proper hourly wage (since you are technically working out of the title of landscaper).

The point I'm making is that this whole leaf clean-up scenario happens every day in your office. If you itemize every task that you are responsible for over a week or a month (depending on your work cycle) and let's just say that if you made a to-do list of everything you would be required to complete in a month, there would be, say, 100 tasks. Now, if you were the leaf raker and you knew you had 100 things to complete before you were able to get paid and you had one month to complete all tasks, I think you would able to schedule each those 100 tasks during the month and complete them accordingly. Whether it took you four hours a day to complete all 100 jobs in the month or 12 hours, as long as you completed the tasks, you should get paid. The problem lies when that glass table breaks. You can negotiate with that homeowner on a price to do the additional work, but that doesn't happen at the office (unless you are paid hourly and get paid overtime). For all of us salaried employees, it's just extra work we need to do each month. Some of it is out-of-title work, meaning either above or below our current level of responsibilities.

I'm not saying that we shouldn't do this extra work, and really, it's in our best interest to do these extra projects (more on this later), but I just want to put the Give Zero F*ck philosophy in context. If you are the type of person that finishes everything on your to-do list in four hours, I don't want you to feel the slightest bit guilty about checking everything off your list and spend the rest of the day doing something productive for yourself. (For ideas on how to use your personal time, see the previous chapter.) In the office, you are not going to get paid extra for cleaning up the broken glass (doing the extra work). You may be lucky and get a bonus at the end of the year, but that usually doesn't come close to all of the extra time spent doing things that aren't in your actual job description, so don't feel like you're cheating anyone because, like it or not, you're the one who got the short end of the stick.

MANAGING YOUR DAY-TO-DAY - THE BASICS

STEP 1 - THE LIST

When I mentioned earlier about creating a to-do list that covers your entire work cycle, I wasn't kidding. Not only will it help immensely with getting a more productive and stress-free life. It also helps you stay organized throughout the day, week & month.

I'm sure you knew that a list helps you stay organized before picking up this book. We use lists to schedule pretty much every task in the month. (I'm going to use a month as the work cycle going forward, probably most offices run on a monthly cycle). By scheduling each task, we'll know exactly how much actual work we have on a given day.

I'd take some time at work and start compiling a list of every task that my "job description" describes. Knowing, full well, that we'll be bombarded with special projects every day. I'd probably use a spreadsheet, like Excel, and list every task down one column (Column A). Then, in Column B, I'd schedule an approximate time of the month that this task should be completed. In column C, I'd assign a time to each task. (This should be the actual time it takes you to complete the job). In column D, I'd assign each task a multiple. Remember a multiple is how long you think your boss or co-workers would take to do a particular job. (or, at least, how long they think it should take you). Then compare that to how long you actually take to do that task. (For example: If a reconciliation takes you an hour and a half to complete. But it takes your boss three to four hours to do the reconciliation, then your multiple is between two and two and a half.) Either be more conservative and use 2 or give zero f*cks and use the two and a half multiple.

I'd also consider making a column for dependents. These are things that are dependent on an event happening. (like receiving a bank statement or somebody having to give you something like an analysis before you can do a reconciliation or something like that). Dependency is a prime example of something that caused you to take longer to complete a task than your boss expected (a double benefit).

I recommend using an electronic document, like an Excel spreadsheet. No list is ever perfect or complete the first time you compile it, you will be updating, revising, and adding to this list regularly. So, don't sweat it on the initial attempt.

Besides your daily and monthly activities, use the list to capture any upcoming projects slated to start during the year. When you are in meetings, and your boss mentions a new project or initiative that your department will be working on soon, put it on the list in the spreadsheet on a separate tab, or you can make a different paper list that you keep with your regular list (if you use paper). This list will come into play when we work on our self-evaluation and document our goals for the coming year. We will talk all about this in later chapters, but keep in mind that being proactive during the year, writing everything down as they are mentioned, will help you at year-end when you compile your self-evaluation and goals for the upcoming year. The best thing that can happen is you are so thorough that you mention goals that your boss actually forgot. You will look like a rock star that can't be easily replaced (and that leads to massive job security).

When in doubt, write it down. It's better to capture too much on the list than not enough. Remember, the list is only for your purpose. It doesn't have to be perfect. It doesn't even need to be good. It just needs to remind you of your daily/monthly tasks and the future goals of the department.

STEP 2 - USING THE LIST

Schedule your daily activities - always have an immediate response to that question, "What are you working on."

Not only does this list help you to be as productive as possible. It also allows you to accumulate free time while getting all of your work done in the allotted time. Remember, you are a zero F*ck-giving superstar in your boss's eyes. The list solves the problem that inadvertently will come up all the time. Well, the more of a micro-manager your boss is, the more you will encounter "the question." The question will come in either an email or just in casual conversation. Either way, you need to be able to answer it without hesitation. So, you appear to be inundated with work.

The email usually goes something like, "This is a hectic week, so give me your hit-list of what you're working on so I can make sure..." This is easy and yet requires more work than the casual conversation because now you have to list everything you are planning to do for the week. Luckily for us, we made a list. So we just need to refer to our list (using the time from the column that factors in the multiple) and send him or her a list of what you are planning to accomplish. Especially with a micro-manager, the more prepared you are, the less they'll feel like they have to micro-manage your work. Trust me, if you really work for someone who micro-manages everything, you'll never really be free of their micro-managing ways, but they will usually back off and let you finish your work.

When I send the list back to my manager, detailing what my department and I will be working on, I always include some unknown variables. These are things that usually happen but may not occur on time or even this week. Often, these are related to the dependent work that can hold up my work. So I'll fill my list with caveats like "I'm going review payroll this afternoon, assuming Hector finishes it by 4 o'clock."

For the other line of questioning, it usually begins with a friendly talk in the morning. How was your night or weekend, blah, blah, blah. "So, what are you working on?" or "What are your plans for today." Knowing that this type of question will come up often and without warning, I always like to refer to the list each morning and jot down a few items on a pad and call it a to-do list. Micro-managers love to see lists. Once you start to rattle off your "to-do's" for the day (after being asked what you're working on) and your boss tells you that he needs you to do some project for him, and you pull out your to-do list and add it to the list, your boss should be much more comfortable leaving you alone to accomplish your work.

This is why I try and make a list as complete as possible, so I can use it to not only keep organized but always have a daily to-do list in the back of my mind. The last thing you want to do is give that blank, deer in the headlights, stare when asked what you are working on. This happens if you are not prepared. You really have to scramble to come up with something quick. A real problem with not being prepared is that in the effort to explain what you're working on that day because you're scrambling, you might come up with something that you really didn't need to do or something that didn't really need to get done - today - but now you are committed.

So please, heed my advice and use a list!

STEP 3 - GO ABOVE AND BEYOND

If you have a good rapport with your boss and find yourself in their office chatting every day, whether it's business-related, or you're just catching up on the night before or weekend, somewhere between how a meeting went that you didn't attend and how is their oatmeal this morning, look over and ask what they are working on. I always like to ask, "Can I help you with that?" or "Do you need a hand with that?" Now, nine times out of ten, they will say no. The way I see it, if they wanted to delegate the responsibility to you, then they probably already would have. But just ask, always. Especially if there is a head-honcho in their office.

Even though this might sound counterintuitive to everything I just mentioned, this is helping you become more valuable to your boss but on your terms. Even if he gave you the project that he was working on and it would take you a few hours, but we know it would probably take him/ her the rest of the day, we just bought ourselves some free time. Also, you now have an excuse for pushing everything on your to-do list back because you are working on a project for the boss.

Your goal to pull off the perfect work-life balance and become outstandingly productive while living the stress-free, zero F*cks lifestyle is to gain everyone's trust. Not only your manager but their manager, your co-workers, IT (this is a big one, more on this later). You do not want anyone questioning you. You want to be known as the trusted super-star of the office. You want anyone to be able to come up to you, show you a problem and you solve it. You want to be the best. The thing you don't want to be is the best employee who doesn't have a free minute in the day.

So offering to help really helps to gain the trust of other people. You just start to be seen as the guy (or gal) that can do anything. Since I know the odds are good that he won't actually give me his work to do, I think it's a good trade-off between any extra work actually received and the good-will I'm creating. Plus, I'm learning new things, which only makes me more valuable.

One last way I go above and beyond the call of duty (at least in my manager's eyes) is whenever he's in the office after hours, I try and stay about an extra half an hour before packing up and leaving. Honestly, unless I've been slacking all day and actually have work to do after hours, I just sit and read, or research something online or watch a YouTube video to learn something

I've been meaning to learn. If anyone walked in, it's after hours, so I'm just taking care of something I needed to take care of but had to wait until after work hours.

As we will learn in the next chapter, my boss tends to value people by the amount of time they put in at the office. So this strategy is perfect for a few reasons. First, I get some personal stuff done. This is usually things I meant to do during the day but got caught up with other things. Secondly, this extra half an hour makes me look much more valuable to my boss (a good talking point when asking for a good raise when having your annual review) and lastly, and one of the most important benefits is that I miss all of the rush-hour traffic by staying an extra half-hour. It probably shaves about 10-15 minutes of time off of my commute, so I don't feel the full brunt of the half-hour.

I'll be the first to say that everyone is replaceable, but you want your manager to think you're almost irreplaceable or at least that it would create havoc in the department if they had to replace you. The more they depend on you to handle shit for them, the less likely they'll want to have to replace you. When you get to that stage, you pretty much have to try and get fired. Even in a down economy, the idea of having to do all the work that they rely on you to do is not something they want to even think about.

You should always try to go over and above when it benefits you, but as we'll learn in the next chapter, sometimes it's the boss that is the over-achiever. This can make your life hell. So I'll give you some examples from my work life, and we'll go over the ways to counter the overachieving boss.

CHAPTER 4 - THE OVER-ACHIEVING BOSS

Does this look familiar? No matter what time you arrive at the office, your boss's car is sitting in the parking lot. No matter what time you leave at night, your boss has his/her head down frantically working on some type of report or some other project. Now, let me give you my experience with what I call the Over-Achieving Boss. In my experience, this person doesn't have 12 hours of work to do each day, so why would they work 12+ hours a day? Again, this is my experience, but I think the answer to that question is really two-fold.

First, as I mentioned earlier, they work as slow as shit. They rose through the ranks by some office-political miracle, and they never really learned how to do work. What I mean here is that they know how to put a report together but instead of taking advantage of modern tools that they have at their disposable, like Excel or Word (or copy and paste… I kid you not) and use these tools correctly, they do everything in the most manual way you can possibly do it. And what pisses me off the most is that I know I've shown them how to do something multiple times (probably dozens of times), but they just don't want to learn. If there was a much better and easier way to do a job, I would make it my priority to learn how to do it more efficiently. In fact, a lot of my "personal time" is spent learning things that make me better at my job. (I like to get more efficient, so I have more personal time during the day, my boss should just try and get more efficient, so he can get his work done on time).

The second reason I feel that my boss is the first one in and last one out each day is that he puts a strong value on the number of hours worked (not the amount of work completed). I believe, at least in my case, that my boss makes pretty damn good money for someone who has a hard time keeping up. What I mean by that is he'll take four hours to complete something that would take a normal person (who uses the technology the way it's supposed to be used) an hour and a half, two hours. I literally worked with a guy that still used a giant 14 column ledger to calculate their work. A paper ledger, a pencil, and an adding machine, then they wonder why things take them three times longer than everyone else.

In my boss's mind, the way to prove to the CEO that he is a team player is to put in the hours. So he thinks that 12-hour workdays make him look like a hard worker (I said hard, not smart), and this perpetual cycle is compounded if the CEO also values time spent in the office as a way to prove that you're "dedicated" and a "good worker."

The fact is, he needs a lot of extra time actually to finish the work. This is partially due to him being a slow and inefficient worker and also because he probably does his fair share slacking off during the day (whether it's reading the newspaper, taking a long lunch or flirting with an office worker). Working slow coupled with his value that more time equals a better, more dedicated employee, compounded by having a CEO who also has a similar belief system (that more time equals good, dedicated employees) creates the perfect storm that I call the Over-Achieving Boss.

A third reason, which is probably not the case in my current situation, but I have seen it many times before, is that the boss just doesn't like being home with his/her family. Maybe they have little kids at home and would rather work an extra hour or two than go home and have to spend time with them. They just sneak in, just in time to tuck them into bed. Or maybe they don't want to spend too much time with their spouse. Maybe they are heading for a divorce and are only staying together for the sake of the children. This is where you may see affairs start to happen. If you do notice your boss getting very "friendly" with someone, then you might want to start looking for another job. Most people can't hide affairs for too long, and once a marriage gets to that point, it's only a matter of time before the divorce.

Trust me, you don't want to work for someone who is going through a divorce. It sucks. Your work-life will suffer, believe me.

GERARD HENRY

HOW TO TELL IF YOU WORK FOR A SELF-PROCLAIMED OVER-ACHIEVER (AND WHAT TO DO ABOUT IT)?

The over-achiever (OA from here on out) values time spent over actual work produced. This is a significant problem when it comes to having a great work-life balance. If you work efficiently and get your required tasks done on time, you are just given more work to fill up the allotted time conjured up by the OA. Conversely, if you work slow and spend 12 hours a day working on various tasks, you look like a Rockstar in the OA eyes. So it's very possible that you, the efficient worker, get more work done every day but leaves on time. And because you leave on time every night, you get a worse review (and raise) than someone who dilly-dallies all day and takes as much time as the OA to get things done (working 10 or 12-hour days). Like I said, the OA values time spent in the office above almost everything else.

If you are not sure if you work for someone who falls in the OA category, here are some typical behaviors and language that OA's tend to display:

- First off, they flat out tell you. Usually, in a phrase like "I went by your desk at 5:05, but you weren't around… I actually had to do something myself (ok, the last part was me responding silently to such a ridiculous accusation). Here the OA basically wants you to know that he/she knows that you left on time and that they wouldn't dream of leaving on time, so think twice next time.

- They tell you a little more subtlety by using phrases such as "clock-watchers" or "5 o'clock express". Here the OA is basically calling out an employee. They probably left on time, and the OA needed them for some reason. But more subtlety, they are letting you know that that this is unacceptable behavior. By calling out someone else, they are also giving you an order. (albeit indirectly because they are most likely a coward and have to rely on emails and indirect messages to get their point across.)

- You get into the office at the standard start time, and you already have two or three emails from the OA outlining his/her day and your day. Or you check your emails in the morning, and there are various emails from the night before 7 o'clock and another at 8 o'clock… etc. These late-night emails will usually have a bunch of people cc'd, so everyone knows how late they work. In their minds, this is dedication.

- The weekend warrior. Certain times during the year, the OA will feel the need to work on the weekends. Most of the time, it's not really necessary, but that doesn't deter them. The more cowardly OA's will drop hints about the weekend like, "I think I'm going to come in on Sunday to finish up." (and if this is really the case it's because he did everything but what he/she was supposed to during the week). So, the OA will drop hints to you, these hints are basically telling you that he/she is putting in some time this weekend and that you should also. (Remember this can be held against you during a review, "Well, Joe Slow came in on four weekends during the summer, and you didn't make an effort." Even if Joe Slow works at a snail's pace, and regardless of whether Joe Slow got a glowing review, the OA will use this against you. In typical OA fashion, everyone in the world will know that they are working over the weekend. Every conversation, every email will reference coming in on Sunday. Remember, this is how the OA defines job security, showing how dedicated he/she is by putting in as many hours as possible…

What can we do to combat some of these extra added work scenarios?

Our best defense in these scenarios is to have a good offense. Our best offense like with the "Please tell me your actions items for the day" question, is to keep a good list. Now this list can be true or just have a bunch of fictitious things on a list that you can spit out at a moment's notice. So, the "I'm coming in on Saturday to work on X, Y & Z," and as they stand there waiting for you to go "What time will you be in, I'm happy to give up half my Saturday and join you in the office for no good reason." Instead, without missing a beat, you spit out "Crap, Saturday? I'm having my annual physical. It took me 3 months to get a Saturday appointment. Sorry…."

So, just like we have to keep a list with all of the monthly duties that we can use when asked to answer the questions "What are you working on?" or "What are the action items you are working on today?", we need to always have one or two weekend scenarios (and probably one or two evening scenarios) that we can immediately spit out when we need to get out of unnecessary hours in the office. Whatever terminology they use, you must have an answer instantly. The more you hesitate, the more it'll appear that you don't really have a game plan or actually have something else to do. Just like you need a to-do list, you also must have a list of things you have to do outside of work. This list should cover a wide range of reasons why you can't stay late, come in on the weekends, work through lunch, travel, or whatever needless thing your co-dependent boss asks of you. These "excuses" are to be used to keep you from wasting your time on completely unnecessary things. This would equate to coming in on a Saturday to (most likely) keep your boss company. If you are following the Zero F*cks philosophy then your work should be pretty much up to date, your boss may think there are open items but you have been managing his / her expectations so it would be a complete waste of time for you to stay late for hours each night or come into the office on the weekend. Unfortunately, this is something that needs to be nipped in the bud, otherwise, your boss will always expect it from you, and that is ridiculous if you are completely up to date on all of your work. Life is too short to waste valuable time sitting in a cubicle.

Now having said that, there are times you will actually need to put in some extra time. And this will work to your advantage. The necessary extra time is where you really do need to accomplish something, usually a big project or something out of the regular course of business. The best extra-work is when your boss is absolutely desperate and didn't finish something vitally important that he/she needed to, and you have to "bail them out." Now you have something to add to your self-evaluation and performance review. We will discuss ways to ace the self-evaluation shortly, but I wanted to mention this now. Like the to-do list and the list of extracurricular activities, you need to keep a record of your accomplishments and regularly update it. Update it every time you do something out of your official job description. You probably won't use every item on the list, but it's better to have too much to write about then scrambling to think of enough accomplishments to write about.

Office politics come into play a lot of the time. Sometimes it doesn't matter how correct you are, it's better to avoid conflict at work. This could become a significant advantage for you. In the next chapter, we will discuss knowing when to hold 'em and when to fold 'em. Choosing your battles… wisely.

CHAPTER 5 - CHOOSE YOUR BATTLES... WISELY

It's almost cliché - pick your battles - but in the business world, it really is in your best interest to choose when to really dig in and fight and when to compromise. I will show you that there are times and ways that you can concede a position and also benefit from that concession. Sometimes it's in your best interest to make a compromise. Let's take a look.

I know it's tough, especially when you know you are correct, to give in on a position where you hold a very strong opinion. You know you are right, your manager (or anyone in the organization) isn't seeing the big picture, and you feel the need to go to war to show them you are correct. You start imagining the PowerPoint presentation you'll put together, highlighting all of the beautiful analysis you prepared in Excel, proving your point. Does any of this sound familiar? I find that the right-hand man (or woman) usually is correct about a lot of things and often get overruled by their managers. Sometimes the manager just doesn't understand or doesn't care enough to spend the time to learn why you are correct, and their logic is flawed. It's enough to drive you crazy, having to concede on a point where you know you are 100% accurate, you have data supporting that assertion, but no one will pay attention long enough to hear you out.

At least that drives me crazy. It's like one year when I was a kid playing baseball in little league. I was playing left field in this game when someone on the other team hit a long fly ball out to left field. I ran over and caught the ball, probably an inch from hitting the ground. That batter was out, I think I started running off the field because that was the third out and I thought the inning was over. Well, the umpire didn't see it that way. He thought that the ball bounced before I caught it, so he called a fair ball. So what was I to do, now the batter is rounding first heading to second. It dawns on me that the umpire didn't think I caught to ball, so in his opinion, the ball is still in play. I had two choices. One I could argue my point right there while the batter rounds second and then third base, effectively getting an in the park home run or I can throw the ball to the shortstop and stop the batter on second for only a double. I know I'm right; I know the batter was out, but somebody in charge of calling the game (the umpire) didn't see it that way. He was 100% wrong, and yet I had to play as if the ball dropped to prevent a home run. I took one for the team as they say. Of course, once the play was over, I furiously argued that I caught the ball, but it didn't matter because the umpire didn't see it that way and he overruled me (there were no iPhones or instant replay back then). I was right, he was wrong, but I just had to deal with it. I had to make a split-second decision to choose NOT to BATTLE the umpire's call and throw the ball to the shortstop. Otherwise, the batter would have scored while I was arguing. My point is, sometimes you have to quell the urge to go to battle for the good of the group or, more importantly - for your sanity.

OPERATION: OFFICE SLEUTH

At work, your goal should be to lead a productive, prosperous, STRESS-FREE life. This is why picking your battles at work is a good idea. Now, I'm not saying you shouldn't push back on things. In fact, you should push back often. Pushing back will benefit you when you choose to concede a point. If you didn't push back when things were incorrect, you wouldn't be as valuable to the organization. Definitely less valuable to your manager. You'd just be seen as a yes-man (or yes-woman). To live the Office Sleuth lifestyle, where we do less work but remain the most productive employee in the department, we need our manager to trust our judgment. Pushing back when you are correct (especially when their logic is incorrect) is essential to getting them to depend on you. So, choosing your battles wisely doesn't mean you should never push back or take a stand and argue your case. It just means let's think for a minute if this augment is really worth your time, will this argument add unnecessary stress to my life that ultimately won't matter to my career (or life) in the grand scheme of things?

When you push back often, not only in your physical department with your manager but at meetings and during presentations, people will begin to expect you to challenge their thoughts and ideas. This is fine as long as you are correct, and as long as your challenge is good for the organization, group, or employee that you're challenging. It's probably in your best interest not to challenge things just for the sake of challenging things. You know you're right, but if it's about something that is entirely immaterial, then who cares? People welcome challenges to their ideas if it will help advance their cause, people hate nitpicking little things just because you can. Think of the grammar police on the internet. You write a fantastic blog post that contains valuable information. Anyone reading it should benefit from the blog post. Then you get that one comment about how you confused past and a past participle verb or some crazy shit like that. Even though that commenter may be correct, it adds absolutely no value to information presented in the blog post (unless, of course, the blog you run is a grammar blog :)

HOW TO BENEFIT FROM CONCEDING.

If the idea of conceding, when you know you are correct, drives you mad, then let's decide right now how you can benefit from conceding. I find that when I have the facts, I can prove why I'm right, but I know there is some reason that my manager does not want to fight this fight anymore. I will definitely get anxious, possibly angry, and definitely not have a stress-free work environment anymore. He is my manager, I report to him, so even though my data shows otherwise, we are going to do what he wants to do anyway. Now I have two choices, I can get stressed and try really hard to change his mind. I can show him all the analysis in the world, but you know, going in, that his decision has been made. Or you can just agree with him.

You want me to agree with him? But you're thinking, "That's not in my nature to just give in and do something that is incorrect, WTF?" Remember, I didn't say that you think he is correct, I just told you to agree with him. Let me set this up for you. You have tried, really hard to convince him that we should (or shouldn't) do something, you have the facts that support your assertion. He knows you are passionate about this. But for some reason, whether it's laziness, or he doesn't want to or doesn't have time to do any more analysis, or, more likely, a political thing in the office, you're not going to change his mind. The definition of "a political thing" is someone else in the office is pressuring him to get something done. Even if his analysis is wrong and it costs the company a few extra dollars, it doesn't matter. That cost is immaterial to the possibility of weakening the relationship between your manager and someone else in the organization (probably his manager). Or maybe he owes someone a favor, or perhaps he's trying to do something now that gets him a favor in the future. Any way you slice it, it's political. It's the game that is played in companies that you don't learn about in textbooks. Knowing this is probably a political move. (and by that I mean, right or wrong, it's getting done the way your manager wants.) How can we gain some political points by conceding our beliefs?

The only person, in this scenario, that we can gain a political point from is our manager. This is not always the case. Depending on who you are dealing with within the organization, you can earn political points with any of them. But in this example, it's our manager that we have to appease (concede what is right for them). The first step is to make your case. You do have to really try and convince him that you are right, show him your analysis, make your case. He has to know that you genuinely believe what you are presenting and that you are passionate in your belief. In his mind, giving up is not an option. You may have to go back and forth a few times with him, each time giving him a reason as to why you are absolutely right. Eventually, he'll come into your office and say something like, "Let's just do it this way, we'll revisit how this is done next month, year..."

That is your cue. At this point, you realize that we are going to do it the way your manager wants. He is aware of your strong feelings about it and is making a concession of his own (revisit how it's done in the future). Now it's your turn to concede. But remember, you are gaining political points with this concession. You will just look at your boss and say, "Ok, no problem." Short and sweet. This accomplishes a few things. First, your boss knows that you were pretty passionate about not doing it (or doing it a different way). He recognizes your concession, knowing that you were passionate and knowing that you might try and argue this point all day. Plus, knowing that he has to do it his way for some political reason, you just relieved a lot of stress from your manager. He was probably feeling a lot of tension, and by you just aligning with him and agreeing to do it his way, he probably feels relieved. Either way, this should cement your position on his team. He probably knows that you are correct. But he doesn't want to spend the time or burn the political points fighting over something that's probably immaterial in the long run. You just have to recognize when you get to the point where continuing to fight is futile. Believe me, I hate giving up when I am correct. But sometimes you have to put a stress-free work environment over a small victory that is meaningless to your future at the company.

Let me summarize this in an example that happened recently. I was working for a company that had different branch locations across the country. In their employment agreements, the managers of these branches had bonus potential each year based on a few criteria related to the performance of their branches. One branch is losing a ton of money, overall, their margins are horrible, and we were strongly considering closing this particular branch. So when it came down to bonuses, I did a quick analysis and using the criteria from this branch manager's employment agreement, I determined what the maximum bonus that he could possibly earn. Remember, this was a quick, down and dirty analysis. But even though some aspects can earn a small amount of bonus, I make the assertion that he doesn't receive a bonus this year, because the branch is losing money (like there's no tomorrow).

I feel this assertion should be obvious to anyone looking at the analysis. The branch is losing a ton of money, so I would think this branch manager should feel lucky to still have a job. But I get a call from the regional manager asking about his guy's bonus. Now my quick analysis put the max bonus at about $2,000 (even though it showed $2,000, I put about six disclaimers explaining why in a more thorough analysis this number would be drastically reduced (probably cut in half). The regional manager explains that this guy, the branch manager feels he's owed about $10,000. After getting off the floor because I fell off my chair when I heard that, I said I'd talk to my manager and see what we can do. Long story short, my analysis, showing the $2,000 owed to this branch manager, was sent by my manager to the regional manager's manager, the VP of operations. Even though I had a half dozen disclaimers saying this number will be drastically reduced if I do a more thorough analysis and shows the P&L at a massive loss for the year, everyone focused on one number, the $2,000.

So I get an email from my manager saying to give payroll the number for his bonus. So I immediately go into my boss's office and explain that the $2,000 was not the amount owed. I still asserted that he shouldn't receive anything, but if he was going to get something, let me do a thorough analysis and come up with the right number (or let's just cut it in half to save the time). I start putting together my analysis when my manager walks into my office and gives me the "Let's just pay him so he doesn't quit, and we'll revisit the bonus plans for next year…" Bingo, that is my cue, "Ok, no problem." I think he realizes I'm right, but he doesn't want to spend all day analyzing and then arguing with the operations team over a few hundred or even a thousand dollars. To him, it's immaterial in the grand scheme of things, and by us, biting our tongues and agreeing, we just banked a couple of political points. One with our manager, one with the VP of operations, and probably one with the regional manager because his branch manager won't quit.

WHEN YOU SHOULD NEVER CONCEDE

Giving in to make your work life stress-free is a good thing occasionally. You have to learn to recognize when it becomes very political, and no matter how correct you are, it just doesn't matter. So when it gets to that point, it's almost always in your best interest to save yourself the trouble, gain a political point or two, and just move on.

When is it never ok to concede? Are there certain times that, unless I'm paid a lot of money to shut up, I would never concede?

Yes. I highly recommend that you don't give in when it involves falsehoods aimed at you personally. Suppose I have my annual performance review, and we have a stark difference of opinion about my accomplishments or abilities. If I'm being honest with myself, then I will never concede the difference. Let me give you an example to help illustrate this point.

I pitched the idea of taking on managing another department in the company. It was a department that should have been set up under the finance group, but because of the logistics, it wasn't falling under the supervision of the finance department. My idea was to split my time. I'd travel to the other location for half the week and manage my home location for the rest of the week. It was a fairly common occurrence that I worked at the other office, so this wasn't really unusual. Where it became unusual was, since the day I pitched the idea, my manager would travel with me to the other location. And from there, he basically took over managing my group. He would set up meetings with them, where I wasn't even included (and I was supposed to be the department head). He would take the girls out to lunch or dinner or out for drinks, again I wasn't included most of the time.

I used to come home and tell my wife how weird it was that he is now so gung-ho on coming with me. And that he's making it almost impossible for me to manage. I don't know if he liked a girl on the other team or felt threatened that I was trying to manage something that wasn't under his direct control, but the whole scenario was just weird. Now, we know that my manager is a complete and total micromanager (**MUCH** more on this later). It's his biggest weakness. Normally, I can exploit this for my own benefit, but here he just straight-up usurped me from managing this team. It was regrettable, too, because I came up with this concept to help me move up a little in the organization. My direct manager's position would be my next logical step for growth at this company, however I doubted he had any plans to go anywhere, anytime soon. So, this was my way of growing my career without interfering with my manager's position or having to leave my current company.

You may remember this from an earlier chapter, but I didn't get close to the increase I thought I'd get for taking on another department. So when my boss shadowed all my trips to the other location and basically took over, I said to myself, my wife and friends, "Ok, I'll let him take on the extra work if he wants. He is the boss." (Plus, I'm not making nearly as much as I thought I'd be making after taking on the extra department.) The more I thought about this new scenario, the better I felt about the way things happened. Instead of me traveling multiple days per week, now he was going to have to travel. I started to feel that things sort of worked out for the best, (assuming I was happy working under a micro-manager with basically zero prospects of growth opportunity). All I can say is this new scenario worked for me, at least until my performance review.

During my performance review, I got my usually glowing (typical Office Sleuth) review. As you will learn shortly, having a system in place to compile your self-evaluation and then using my techniques for the actual performance review usually leads to good results. But when it came to the other department, he said something like, "That didn't work out too well, so I had to step in…" I literally spit out a big gulp of unsweetened iced tea when he said that. The hilarious thing was that he was actually surprised by my reaction. He gave me an otherwise glowing review, a good raise, and a bonus, so I guess he just thought it would be an easy review. I'd just agree, sign it and we'd go about eating our lunch. I always find it awkward to have a performance review in a restaurant. It's the one conversation I have all year that I don't want a bunch of strangers, sitting around my table, to be able to hear. But my manager loves doing reviews out at lunch (probably to avoid confrontations during the review). Anyway, I immediately challenge him on this point, I said exactly what I've been telling my family and friends. I found it really weird that you had to come with me every time I traveled, you'd have meetings where I wasn't even included, you go out for lunch, drinks… etc.

Now to say he was taken aback would be an understatement. He had no recollection of anything I said. Let me say this, during my career, and in my personal experience, 100% of micro-managers do not think they micro-manage. Honestly, most of them believe the complete opposite and get very offended when you call them out for being a micro-manager. So, the fact that I basically called him a liar because of the way he wrote up my performance review (that it didn't work out too well) went unnoticed. He was most distraught because I called him a micro-manager. That phrase really offended him, and now he is arguing with me over my use of the phrase.

Most people would have just signed the otherwise great review and moved on, but your annual review goes into your permanent personal file, and the last thing I wanted in there was a sentence about me - pretty much - failing at a task. Especially when I was 100% certain that I didn't. It was due to his micro-managing, and that was what I would change my review to say if he didn't remove or replace the line (He ended up changing the wording to something like, I helped him manage the new department).

Fine. But again, there is no way I'd let someone accuse me of failing, especially in a report that would go into my personal file. Unless it was true, and if it really was true, I think I'd be aware enough to recognize this and just move on. This was not true, and I was never going to concede this point. Funny thing, after this whole discussion about micro-managing and changing my review, he still does not believe he is, in any way, a micro-manager.

Do you work for a raging micro-manager? We'll answer that question in the coming chapters.

CHAPTER 6 - THE AFTER-VACATION SYNDROME

Here is a weird scenario that I often encounter. It's weird because you would expect the exact opposite to happen. What am I talking about? I call it the After-Vacation-Syndrome (AVS). You're probably thinking, "What is AVS?"

After-Vacation-Syndrome is when your boss goes on a vacation. Unlike any sane person, they just can't get enough of the place. The whole time they are away, it seems like they have to call you, email you, text you, send F*cking smoke signals, whatever means they have to contact you. Basically, they are doing everything they can to act like they are the perfect company man (or woman) and have this need to keep on working through vacation. If I didn't usually sit within earshot of my boss and couldn't walk past and actually see that his office was empty and the lights were off, I wouldn't even think he left the office (let alone the country.)

I may speculate why someone would do this, maybe they need the senior management team to think that work is more important than taking his / her kids to Disney or more important than spending a romantic week with his / her spouse on some beautiful beach in a tropical paradise. Whatever the reason, I give Zero F*cks, but where I start to give a F*ck is when they return.

First of all, let me start by saying the entire week or two that he is "away" (at least physically) I have assumed his responsibilities. My responsibilities haven't changed, so I still have all of them, plus any special projects from the "c suite" now falls in my lap. I don't mind this, I keep a detailed list, I work a lot faster than I let on, in fact, this will be one of my talking points on my annual review. The problems always seem to start when they are back in the office. They may have a great tan, but they look anything but relaxed and well-rested. In fact, they look tense and outright pissed off. I don't know if they are coming back to a pile of work that someone left them, or they are just pissed that they are back in work or maybe they had a fight with their significant other, who knows. All I know is that when my boss goes away on vacation, it's always the same thing when he gets back.

Before I tell you about how my boss acts upon return from his glorious vacation, let's take a minute to think of how a normal person should act. They have been away for a week or two, whether relaxing on a beach in the Caribbean, sightseeing in Europe, Disney with the kids, or just staying home and relaxing. Any way you slice it, they should be relaxed and happy that they were away. Maybe even a little anxious to get back to work. You'd expect that their first morning back would be a little lazy for them, chit-chatting as they walked around the office, telling everyone about the great adventures they had over the past week, or at least a big smile on their face. Even though there will be a lot of catching up to do, they were on a nice vacation somewhere. And this should have given him the chance to relax and recharge. The last thing I'd expect to see is a tense, pissed off person (more so than a normal morning) come into the office saying nothing to anyone while walking to their office. Instead of a "Good Morning," he closes the door, and that is the last I see of him for a good part of the morning.

At least until the inquisition starts.

LET'S CATCH-UP.

After a few hours of being behind closed doors, my phone rings, of course, it's my boss, and he wants to catch-up right away. Now, this is fine if they really are interested in catching up, but I walk into their office, and it's literally like being on trial. I'm sitting down looking at my obviously pissed-off boss, and he proceeds to interrogate me about the details of everything that happened, every minute, during the week. I try my best to bring him around, asking him about the vacation, how his kids liked Mickey Mouse, ...etc. No luck. He immediately redirects the meeting back to what happened at work during the week. I might be crazy, but I really think that he was pissed because I was free to do my own work without him being there to micro-manage me. Even though he was on vacation. Have you worked with someone like this? Either that or they are so far behind, they start to delegate work like there's no tomorrow.

That's when we get into the to-do phase of this interrogation. What seems like coming out of the blue is a well-orchestrated to-do list that needs to get accomplished immediately. I honestly feel that he was thinking this list throughout the entire vacation. And literally got to work an hour early because he couldn't wait to have this conversation with me.

HOW TO HANDLE THE LIST

Now being of the Zero F*cks mentality, I give zero F*cks about this list. I am uber-efficient with my own work, primarily due to my own lists, plus the extra multiple that I've assigned to each task. His extra work really doesn't faze me. If anything, it affords me more excuses about why certain things may be taking longer than usual. When you sit through this tirade and get the inevitable list of extra to-dos, don't sweat it. It will actually help you in the long run in a few ways.

You have an excuse for why certain work is taking longer than usual. Deadlines may be getting missed (depending on how much actual work you are given.)

Make him/her prioritize any tasks whose deadlines are in conflict with each other. This prevents the questions of why 'x' isn't done because they made 'y' the priority.

After unloading the massive to-do list, the micro-manager in him or her should be satisfied for a few days. This should keep them off your back for a while, aside from the occasional "Is 'y' ready for review?"

If you are doing work that is normally above your paygrade, then write it down on your accomplishment list. You should definitely bring this up during your annual review.

If your boss is in an especially bad mood. And you are really taking the brunt of his tirade (for no reason other than he has been out of the office for a week), then use these extra assignments, along with a liberal dose of the multiple to give yourself whatever free time you need during the next few days. You have the perfect excuse (all of the extra work to help your boss catch-up) and remember, it's not your fault he took a vacation.

Personally, I can't wrap my head around the idea that you can take a vacation, typically to unwind or recharge the batteries, and come back even more stressed out than before you left. If that's what it takes to get to the C-suite, then I don't know if it's even worth it. I know everyone has their own priorities, so you may feel differently, but life is too short to have to deal with that.

Now that we've been talking about vacations, what about when you go on vacation?

YOUR VACATION - A BLESSING OR A CURSE?

So let's flip the coin and think about when you need to take a vacation. There are a few reasons you should definitely schedule a vacation, I'm sure you can think of a lot of others:

- You want to take a trip somewhere
- You have things to do around the house or locally

- A family member (or you) might need a medical procedure
- Work on a project or hobby (e.g., write a book)
- Just some time off to unwind and recharge the batteries.

The list can go on forever, but notice the one thing I didn't mention? When it comes to vacations, I would never mention - work. By work, I mean the job you work full time that is now paying you to take a vacation. I often use some time off to work on a project (of my own) like writing a book, creating a training program, painting the house…etc. This is all work, but it's personal, it's not from your job.

You definitely need to take a vacation for at least your own sanity, but one thing you must think about is who might do your work (or who will pick up any special projects while you're gone.) Normally, this isn't too important, but as an Office Sleuth, this becomes relevant.

The last thing you want is someone who is trying to make a name for themselves, work at light speed to get things done. Anything that might disrupt your multiple is a bad thing. What I mean is this. If a project that your manager gives you takes you two hours to complete (at full speed). And you work in a multiple of two (so you leave a two-hour buffer and don't submit the project for four hours), the last thing you want is someone who is totally gung-ho finishing this project in three hours. Granted, this is still 50% slower than you could get the job done, but they are eating into your multiple by 50%.

OPERATION: OFFICE SLEUTH

Assuming they do the job correctly and the manager is conscious of how much time it normally takes you, then we may have an issue going forward. The gung-ho employee just cut 50% off of your multiple. (Remember the "parcel delivery company" story, once management witnesses the work getting done in a shorter time, then they will always expect that.)

What can you do to prevent this from happening before you go away on vacation?

The first thing I would make sure is that your work is up to date. You can't necessarily stop your manager from having a project that he'll need help finishing. But your work is undoubtedly within your power to get done. (At least as up to date to possible.) The first thing I would do is go to my to-do list for the month and highlight everything that is needed (or due) during the vacation week. Once you identify the list for the week, then you need to work on getting these items done. Here is the trick of how you should accomplish this feat. Get everything done, working at your normal pace, without using any multiple. You aren't really working any faster than you normally do but you are spending the whole day working. Remember, the last thing we need to happen is for someone else to touch our work and do it faster than we've been doing it (or at least faster than we've been handing it into our boss). It can really affect our multiple (buffer), and then life at work might start to suck.

Do not tell your manager that you are finishing everything while working this week. This is something you will talk about right before you leave on the day before you start your vacation.

(E.g. If you are taking a full calendar week off before you leave on Friday night, sit down with your manager and go over everything that was required for the next week. Tell him where he can find all of the schedules and work that you prepared (or just send them to him.)

If you weren't able to get something done, maybe you are waiting for information that won't be available until next week. Have one of your direct reports work on it during the week of your vacation. This serves two purposes. First, you will go over the steps and procedures with that person. Since it's their first time performing the task, they probably will take a bit longer than you. I'd tell them to double and triple check the work before sending it to senior management (stress accuracy over speed). As you brief your manager before your vacation, explain what you finished and tell him that 'so and so' will be completing this task on Wednesday or Thursday (make sure that you set expectations and give them a little buffer as well). This is the second reason you want to make sure that you arrange for your work to get done, you are the one scheduling it, so the manager isn't directly involved from start to finish. He receives the project when it's complete. So even if your employee follows your notes to the letter and finishes a job that would take you two hours in three (where you use a 2x multiple), the manager won't know precisely how long it took the employee. Also, the employee has their own work to do, so your project will probably get done in between their work. They probably won't stop everything and work straight through your project. This helps to muddy the water when it comes to keeping track of how much time it took to complete your project.

Manager projects can also boost your worth to the organization. The last thing a busy manager wants to do is train someone else to take on tasks that you perform flawlessly. Chances are that your employee will make a few mistakes if it's a reasonably complicated project, or they will have a bunch of questions for the manager. This typically annoys busy managers and will make them long for you to get back to work. So they can just hand off a project, and they know four hours later it will be sitting in their inbox, complete and correct. I remember one time a woman was out on maternity leave. She took her eight weeks (or was it ten?) and then worked out that she would be working from home three days a week for a couple months. While working remotely from home, she was very responsive, if you didn't sit by her office, you never would have known that she was out of the office, working from home. One day the manager needed something, and it was work that required this woman to be physically in the office to perform. The bottom line, her manager had to try and figure out how to do the job. He got terribly frustrated and later that day decided that she needed to be working in the office at least three days a week. This made things harder for her because daycare was one of the main reasons she worked out the three days home two days in the office schedule in the first place.

The last thing you want is a frustrated manager, this makes being an Office Sleuth much more difficult. The funny thing is, you can get less work done if it's done the first time correctly. I know my manager would rather get a project in four hours, that is prepared accurately and completely, then getting something rushed in two hours that needs revisions. Even though it only takes you two hours to prepare the work, you still leave yourself a buffer to double-check that everything is correct. And (probably) more importantly, you have an extra two hours to think about whether or not you forgot anything. Sometimes after giving some thought about a project, something pops into your mind that you might have forgotten or thought of something new. The funny thing about the multiple and the time buffer is that your subconscious mind never fully let's go of the project until you click send on the email. It's like your brain still owns the project until you pass it along to the next person. I usually think of things during this time, and then I'm happy I didn't rush it out the door.

Thinking of something new to add to a project or thinking about a new way to look at something is a great way to add even more time to your multiple. The caveat here is that you always want to run this new idea by the person who assigned you the work. For example, if something takes you two hours to complete (at full speed), and you use a multiple of 2x, then you normally wouldn't send the completed project to the manager for approximately four hours. But if you think of something that might have been missing or maybe there is a new or better way to analyze something, you have a chance to either add to the time the project takes (and use the same multiple) or make it seem like it will increase the time it takes (and increase the multiple.) As mentioned above, you absolutely have to run this new idea by the manager who assigned the project.

There are two reasons you must always do this. First, it gets the managers' buy-in', some brilliant ideas are lost on a manager who is set in their ways. Some managers just don't want to learn or think about new things and added a new analysis to a report that would cause them to have to think about something new, explain the new analysis to others, and this might actually change the ideas of the past. Some people welcome new and improved ideas, while others rather not 'rock the boat.' This is why manager 'buy-in' is absolutely critical.

The second reason you must run this new idea past the manager who assigned the project is to help with our Office Sleuthing. After getting his or her 'buy-in,' we need to make them aware of all of the extra steps we're going to have to take to perform this additional analysis. Now, these new steps might replace old steps, so it nets no extra time to complete, but they don't need to know that. More realistically, it will increase the amount of work the project will take. So I need to make them aware of this, so it doesn't eat into my multiple. There are two scenarios you will encounter, and depending on which scenario is relevant, you will need to mention one of them to the manager. The first is that there is more work to do and you want to give them an idea of how much extra work is involved (on your part), so they can set their expectations (and you can readjust the total time, so it factors in the same multiple, and you gain additional time.) The second scenario is that is doesn't actually take you any more time to get the job done. The new analysis is replacing the old analysis, so the entire project still takes two hours (in our example). Unless the manager is pretty savvy on what's involved, they probably won't realize this and nor should they. They have enough work on their plates, or at least they have enough to keep them looking thoroughly busy twelve hours a day, and most managers will not really care what you need to do to accomplish a task. So you give the appearance of a lot of extra work, thus increasing the potential multiple.

Let me close this chapter with an example of how these two scenarios should play out. In the first scenario, the time the project takes to complete actually increases. So let's say for this example, the project goes from two hours to two and a half hours to actually complete. Now we use a multiple of 2x, so the manager should expect this project in about five hours now. We explained the extra work (factoring in our multiple) and bought us an extra half hour (extra half hour of actual work at a multiple of 2x buys us an extra half hour). In the second scenario, the new analysis replaces the old analysis. It really doesn't take us extra time to perform the task, but we still explain all of the extra work involved without really explaining that it only replaced an older analysis, so the whole job takes the exact same amount of time. Since we are explaining the 'extra' work only, we can slightly increase the multiple a little (you have to be the judge here), but maybe it goes from 2x to 2.25x or even 2.5x. Effectively buying us another half hour (to an hour) - don't get greedy.

In this example, you came up with a procedure to improve a project (now your manager most likely will take all of the credit, unless they are confident and want to shine a light on their great employees). But at least in your manager's eyes, you are making yourself more and more valuable (and this will play a vital role in our ultimate goal (stay tuned). At the same time, we just used this new procedure to buy us some additional personal time. For me, this is a win-win scenario, either way. Your manager is happy and recognizes your potential (whether he keeps that to himself or not really depends on the manager), and you give the appearance of being an extra hour busier (again, at least in your manager's eyes.)

In the next chapter, we'll take a look at the warning signs you'll want to identify to see if your manager is a raving micro-manager.

CHAPTER 7 - WHAT IS A MICRO-MANAGER

I've worked with my fair share of micro-managers. Here I am, a professional. I am supposed to be capable of accomplishing the tasks at hand. Yet my boss feels compelled to check every report and PowerPoint slide I prepare. I've worked with people that wanted to check every email I sent to particular people. Not only does it waste a tremendous amount of time, but how am I supposed to get anything done? Or thinking of the bigger picture, how am I going to grow as an employee? And how the hell is he supposed to finish his work? (It seems he'd rather work 12 hours a day and be "in control," micro-managing everything he possibly can.)

Here I am, the one who is giving the presentation and my boss has to "correct" every slide. Except there was nothing wrong with the slides in the first place, it just wasn't the way he (or she) would have wrote it. So they have to reword every slide in the deck, basically "correcting" it to their style.

He'll tell the entire senior management team that you "own" a project. They should contact you for the next steps to complete the project, but then he tells you exactly how to run it. He emails people, sets up meetings, tells you when and who to send schedules and templates — all on a project that you are supposed to own.

Most of the time, the biggest micro-managers are people who get promoted into a new role but who cannot, for the life of them, let go of their old position. I've worked in finance my whole career. I've seen people get promoted to say, CFO, but cannot let go of the controller's responsibilities they once performed. As if no one can do the role as well as them. Now you might be saying if they weren't that good at their jobs, they wouldn't have gotten promoted? I can tell you straight-up that most promotions are political. Often the best candidate isn't the one hired. Maybe it's the one who works 12 hours a day and continuously calls the office on their vacation? A lot of those people work the hours for recognition to look stellar in senior management's eyes. Or that it takes them twice as long to finish a task. Either way, they might not be as good as they seem.

If you are the main drinking buddy of the president of the company (and you are at least partially qualified), you will probably get the promotion before someone who is definitely better qualified but finishes his work on time, cares more about going home to his family than spending an extra 2-3 hours in the office looking busy or hanging out until 10 o'clock drinking.

If you work for a micro-manager, there is a good chance that they do not feel 100% confident in their current role, so they try and hang onto the last position where they felt in control. (And if any of this sounds familiar, then that role is probably yours.)

Unfortunately, someone who micro-manages diminishes their position with the company because they cannot let go. They continuously do work that is beneath their pay grade, plus they won't allow you to flourish in your role because their hands are in everything you are supposed to be doing. When someone is promoted and finds a competent replacement, the healthy dialogue should go something like this:

BOSS; "I NEED THIS PROJECT DONE IN THREE WEEKS FROM TODAY."

YOU; "OK," THEN YOU ASK ANY PERTINENT QUESTION UPFRONT, SO YOU KNOW EXACTLY WHAT YOU NEED TO DO.

BOSS; "PLEASE LET ME KNOW RIGHT AWAY IF YOU HAVE ANY QUESTIONS OR IF YOU ARE HAVING A PROBLEM GETTING INFORMATION FROM SO AND SO."

YOU; "OK, NO PROBLEM."

Now, if you don't get the project done in three weeks and haven't communicated this effectively to your manager ahead of time, then maybe you do need to be micro-managed. But if after three weeks, you forward the first draft to your manager so he can review, he may offer some constructive criticism or some comments to clean-up and finish the project, but for those three weeks he wasn't up your ass because he had his work to do and he trusted you to complete the project - that is how a healthy working relationship should function.

An easy way to tell if you work for a micro-manager is if the conversation about the project due in three weeks goes something like this:

BOSS; "I NEED THIS PROJECT DONE IN THREE WEEKS FROM TODAY."

YOU; "OK," THEN YOU ASK ANY PERTINENT QUESTION UPFRONT, SO YOU KNOW EXACTLY WHAT YOU NEED TO DO.

BOSS; "PLEASE LET ME KNOW RIGHT AWAY IF YOU HAVE ANY QUESTIONS OR IF YOU ARE HAVING A PROBLEM GETTING INFORMATION FROM SO AND SO."

YOU; "OK, NO PROBLEM."

BOSS; "NOW SEND OUT THE TEMPLATES TO EVERYONE AND TELL THEM WE NEED THEM BACK BY FRIDAY."

BOSS; "MAKE SURE I'M CC'D ON EVERY EMAIL RELATED TO THIS PROJECT. I NEED TO STAY IN THE LOOP."

Two hours later:

BOSS; "I'VE PUT 14 MEETING REQUESTS ON YOUR CALENDAR FOR NEXT MONDAY, WE'LL MEET WITH EVERYONE INVOLVED INDIVIDUALLY."

BOSS; "NO, A CALL WON'T WORK FOR ME. I NEED TO SIT FACE AND FACE AND DISCUSS THE NUMBERS."

Two weeks later:

BOSS; "FOLLOW-UP WITH THEM, MAKE SURE WE HAVE THE LATEST THING."

YOU; "WE HAVE THE LATEST THING, THEY SENT IT LAST FRIDAY."

BOSS; "WHY DIDN'T THEY CC ME, SEND IT TO ME NOW AND TELL THEM TO CC ME ON EVERYTHING."

BEFORE YOU CAN TELL THEM TO CC THE BOSS...

BOSS TO SO AND SO; "PLEASE MAKE SURE YOU CC ME ON EVERYTHING AND FORWARD THE LATEST THING TO ME."

BOSS; "I THINK WE'RE BEHIND ON THIS PROJECT..."

In this example, it's very easy to see that your manager is a classic micro-manager. No matter what they say to you in person, this manager has micro-managing tendencies. In this case they either, don't trust anyone could do the job without them, or they are insecure and can't be out of the loop for a second or they won't know what's going on, or maybe they trust you but (in their minds) they know that no one would do this job as good as they would do it. Remember this manager probably used to do your job. A classic sign of a micro-manager is that they cannot let go of work they used to do. His inability to let go of his work prevents you from doing your job, plus it prevents them from fully engaging in their jobs (because in their minds, this project must get done and without them, it just won't).

I've even worked for someone who used Lotus 123 (now this is circa 2006). Now in case you don't know, Lotus 123 was the main spreadsheet program in the eighties (and maybe early nineties), before Excel became the mainstream spreadsheet. As someone who has worked in a financial capacity since the mid-nineties, I cut my teeth on Excel. I love Excel and would call myself an Excel power user. I was working on an engagement for this manager (the one who loved Lotus 123). Luckily for me, this wasn't my regular manager, I was working on this one engagement with him (it was an annual engagement, probably two months a year). He had all of these schedules in Lotus and come to think of it before I began this engagement, I needed the IT department to install the Lotus program on my computer. That is how outdated it was. Nobody even had the program anymore. Of course, I wanted to get these worksheets into the new millennium, so I converted everything I did into Excel. Like I said, I worked with Excel for years (like everybody in the world) and felt it was necessary to convert everything. Mainly, because I was the one who had to work with and update all of the schedules for the engagement, he would only need to review the finished, printed product, so I didn't think converting the worksheets to Excel would be a problem.

Boy, was I wrong!

I had to come into work on a Saturday and re-do all of the schedules using Lotus 123. Even though he would never be the one who prepared the schedules, the thought of not having them in Lotus just blew his mind. I'm not sure what the exact problem was, but I narrowed it down to two possibilities. One, he created all of these schedules in Lotus and his mind, nobody could do it better than he did, and no matter how much more excel could do, he couldn't handle even the idea of not using his Lotus schedules. Or, he was just lazy and didn't want to learn how to use Excel. He would continue using a program that (by all accounts in my career) has been obsolete for over a decade. Either way, the idea of change, in any capacity, just pushed him off the deep end.

How can you be sure if your manager is a micro-manager? The following list contains some tell-tale signs that you work for one. (And please give some thought to your work philosophy. If you show signs of being a micro-manager, read through the suggestions for the solution) Remember, there is a big difference between being a fully engaged manager vs. being a micro-manager. (As we'll discuss in the next chapter.)

SIGN 1: THEY HAVE TROUBLE SEEING THE BIG PICTURE

A manager (or leader) should be managing the big picture. They shouldn't get bogged down in the minute details of every little thing that everybody is working on at every minute of the day (or of a project). A micro-manager would rather spend their day wrapped up in meetings that their staff is more than adequate to handle. They waste a lot of time performing low-priority tasks with irrelevant results. They tend to be very detail-oriented and will spend an excessive amount of time reviewing reports to correct tiny, immaterial details rather than focusing on the overall big picture.

Examples: The recently promoted manager from the project above that would not let his replacement work independently on the project, felt compelled to be included in every email, every meeting, every minute detail of the project. Or the manager who spends all day reviewing a staff's work papers to come up with a couple of immaterial dollar adjustments, formatting changes, or some other thing that is a complete waste of time for a manager at that level. (E.g. If a highly compensated manager spends two hours reviewing schedules only to have a staff member reclass a $39 item, it just cost the company a lot more than $39 to reclassify a very insignificant amount. Or you get the micro-managing, grammar police, manager that will spend hours reviewing something, and the only notes that come back are grammatical changes or some other immaterial BS.) This is the manager who cannot just give you back something and say = "good job." They have to correct something, even if it's only a misplaced comma on a note you made to yourself. It's as if they feel without them writing notes (corrections) they are not doing their jobs, no matter how immaterial the changes are.

Solution: The primary skill for a good manager is to know when they need to step in and when they should let the staff do their jobs. I find when people get promoted; they need to learn what is required of them (in their new roles). What are their priorities now? They need to trust their employees can perform their workload independently (until there is a reason that they can't - if that is the case, it's time to step in and fully engage with them, to help them grow into their new roles - and, if that doesn't work, they might have to find new employees)

Now, these solutions need to come from within, but you can try and make mention of some things in conversation to see if it sinks in. You might say something like, "I know you are busy with project X, let me manage this other project, and I'll deliver the first draft by Thursday. I'll let you know right away if I need your help." You are showing him that you want to alleviate his stress of project X, letting him focus exclusively on that project, but what you are doing is taking the first step to try and get this micromanager off your ass and hopefully, they start to trust you can handle things without them.

SIGN 2: THEY ARE THE BOTTLENECK

This is another widespread trait among micro-managers. They need to approve everything. Even things that are multiple levels below their pay grade, they need to review before you can do the next step. Approving work takes on a good amount of their day, and if they are out of the office unexpectedly, work can stop because people are waiting for approvals. It wastes a lot of time for the manager and the employee that has to wait for the manager to approve everything.

Examples: I've worked with a high level, senior manager that wanted to review account payable every day. Accounts payable was probably three levels below where he should be spending his time. If there is a significant issue then definitely, get involved. But to review the accounts payable details for almost an hour every day, when you have multiple levels of people who should be reviewing it, is a complete waste of time for this manager. But as we know, with micro-managers, they seem to have a hard time letting go of anything. This isn't the worst thing when he's in the office. Sure, it wastes a lot of time that he should be spending on high-level strategic work, but if he's going to spend one of the twelve hours that he's in the office reviewing AP, then that is up to him. But when he is out of the office, the AP process comes to a grinding halt. Of course, I can review AP (I always do when he schedules time off), but when he is working remotely or sick, it's off my radar. The accounts payable manager will usually come to me towards the end of the day, asking me to approve the AP run.

It's no big deal, but if he relinquished the task and allowed AP to be reviewed according to a hierarchy, we'd never have the bottleneck in the first place. The hierarchy for AP might be something like the accountant reviews AP. If the accountant is out, the senior accountant reviews AP, then the accounting manager, then the controller, then finally, if the entire department has the flu, the senior manager would need to get involved. It becomes the exception rather than the rule. Plus, he freed up about an hour a day.

Solution: Define their current role. A team leader needs to lead. They must oversee and manage people who do their old jobs (not do their past jobs them self). They must trust that people who now are working in the capacity of their last position are fully capable of handling the tasks that they (the manager) used to do. They should be involved in the training process, but once a new employee is trained, they need to cut the apron strings and then manage and lead their team. They need to train their replacement and then let go.

SIGN 3: THEY NEED TO BE CC'D ON EVEN THE MOST MINOR OF EMAILS

Like we mentioned earlier, micro-managers hate to be out of the loop. I don't know if it's insecurity, or they can't just delegate work without remaining 100% involved, but either way, it makes for a very inefficient work environment.

Examples: When you are working on a project with someone in the organization, but your manager feels compelled to be copied on every email. Inevitably, the following will happen to some degree. You'll be communicating with your counterpart on the phone, through Skype, and email. Your micro-managing boss wants to be cc'd on every email for this specific project – all of them. But while you were talking on the phone with your counterpart, he says that he will forward you something in an email. You receive the email (your boss was cc'd because he told everyone to cc him on every email related to this project). Now your boss opens up the email, but he wasn't on the phone conversations, so he has no idea what he's looking at. He calls you into his office to explain the email. So, now you are spending a half-hour explaining what's in the email to your boss.

Meanwhile, you should be working on the project for that half an hour. So the whole team's efficiency suffers because the manager cannot let go and let you do your job. Or suppose he understands what is in the email, maybe it's some preliminary numbers that they send over to get you started on something. The boss begins reviewing the numbers, not knowing that this is a preliminary schedule, and before you know it, your boss calls their boss, and now it's a big shit show (technical term). Now I am forced to have a one-hour conference call to discuss a schedule that was well understood to be some preliminary data because my boss forwarded the preliminary schedule to people who immediately start questioning it.

Or a scenario like this, for every email that my counterpart and I send to each other, I get an email from my boss asking me stupid questions about the last email — basically doubling my workload.

Solution: They need to reevaluate their email policy. They need to trust you can finish a project. Maybe you take the project up to a certain point before he gets involved. At least that way, you'll have some peace to get it partially complete before he swoops in and micro-manages. Unless there is a significant reason that he needs to be so involved (like you completely f*cked up the last project), there is a good chance that you can talk him off the ledge and get him to back off his current email policy. Start with, ***"Until I get to the first draft."*** If he can learn to trust you halfway, then maybe the next project, he'll trust you some more and won't feel the need to be cc'd on all of your emails.

SIGN 4: THEY SUSPECT EVERYBODY IS WASTING TIME AND REQUIRE EVERY EMPLOYEE TO GIVE THEM REGULAR UPDATES

Most micro-managers need constant reminders of what everyone in their departments is working on. We already spoke about the importance of the list and how it will help you field the dreaded, *"What are you working on?"* question. But I find this happens more frequently when they are going to be out of the office for some time. Maybe they are spending a few days at your company's distribution center or corporate headquarters, or perhaps they are visiting a customer or even going on vacation. They need to know what everyone is working on and what their plans for the next week are. I usually get an email that goes something like, "Send me a list of the team's action items for the next week, month…whatever timeframe. Send it to me by lunch, and I'll review, and we'll sit down this afternoon to discuss."

Examples: Probably, one of the worst cases of this was a newly minted CFO who was hired directly out of public accounting. Now for those who don't know about public accounting, as a public accountant, everything you do boils down to something called **billable hours**. The way these billable hours are tracked, so they can be billed to the clients, is something called **the timesheet** (or the **dreaded timeshee**t if you are still in public accounting, but it will be downgraded to just a time sheet as soon as you leave public and don't need to fill one out anymore). The timesheet captures everything you do every day so you can determine which clients are billed for billable work. If you work fifteen minutes on a client answering his question on the phone, you put fifteen minutes of billable time on the time sheet. Next, you work an hour on a tax return for a different client; you put it on the timesheet, you spend three hours reviewing audit work papers for another client, yep it goes on the timesheet. It's a very tedious task, plus the most challenging part is explaining any non-billable time you are spending each day. Trust me, in public accounting, the long hours during tax season, the travel, the pain in the ass audit engagements all suck, but the real reason most people leave public accounting is the time sheet (well, that and the money when a big client offers to double your salary to come and work for them, that helps).

So this fresh, new CFO decided that the best way to figure out what everybody spends their time on each day was to have everyone in the office fill out a timesheet every day for a month. Was I dreaming? Is this what they refer to as a night terror? WTF? This sucks. The funny thing was that even though I was taking a walk down memory lane and reliving past nightmares, I didn't seem to mind it as much as everyone else (those who never worked in public accounting). It became a large document with stretched out time frames and very little busywork. It's almost as if everyone traveled to the future, read this book, then went back in time and added a multiple to every job they do. Needless to say that the timesheets were worthless documents because it didn't represent reality. It was a colossal waste of time, and it sounded the alarm to everyone in the finance department that the new CFO was a raving micro-manager. This was just the beginning. I will share more of the misadventures of this new CFO in the following examples.

Solution: They need to trust that the work is getting completed, timely. Everyone is doing their part, even if it's not exactly how the micro-manager would do it. He needs to look at the big picture rather than the minutia of every task that an employee works. In the above example, the public accounting mindset will fade away on most people (not all) but most. The time it takes to get out of that mindset is different for everyone.

I'm sure there is at least one person in the world that loves filling out their timesheets (probably a micro-manager ;-).

SIGN 5: THEY GET PISSED WHEN EMPLOYEES MAKE DECISIONS WITHOUT RUNNING IT BY THEM FIRST

You know you're working for an extreme micro-manager when they say that you have the authority to make decisions. (and this was noted in writing on an annual review). They still get pissed when you don't run everything by them. It's almost like they want to sound like a great leader during the review process. (we'll cover self-evaluations and reviews a little later). When in reality, they do not want to relinquish control of anything. Even the smallest details, they have to approve. Now, not only is this a completely inefficient way to run a department, but it also indirectly tells everyone in the department that the manager does not trust them. At least they do not trust your judgment; they know that you won't steal paperclips, but all decisions must be run by them first.

Example: One of the most baffling examples comes during a tragedy in my department. I had a senior accountant that was undergoing treatment for a medical issue. We were all very supportive and gave her the time she needed to undergo the procedure and then recover (all including the newly minted CFO). We were all in agreement that this was the right thing to do, and frankly if anyone thought otherwise, they probably have mental issues. So the employee underwent surgery to take care of the problem. After surgery, she spent some time in the hospital recovering. So, my group, the accounting department, decided to send her a fruit basket (you know the ones where they dip fruit in chocolate). So I used my credit card, ordered a nice basket, and we sent it to the hospital. I didn't go to the C-suite and ask the CFO if he wanted to be involved, we just added his name to the card.

At the end of the month, when I was submitting my expense report, I put the fruit basket on the report with the description of why I bought it. The CFO read though my expenses and got freaking pissed. You would have thought that I just embezzled a box of jumbo paper clips because he was visibly pissed off. So, I called him out on it, saying we just wanted to get the employee something to help her recover, and if it was too much of a problem, then I'll pay for it out my own pocket. At that point, I'm not sure if he saw the light or realized he was a freakin moron, but then he started back-pedaling. He goes something like, "Oh, I just thought if you came to me, we could have gotten her a bigger basket."

I mean, really. You just had a conniption over buying a sick employee a $60 fruit basket? It may not be a real business decision, but I'll never forget his reaction. It just blew me away.

The need to wait for the manager's approval for every little decision smothers the department. It tells everyone that they are not trusted and prevents a team from flourishing. The more the organization grows, the less control they have. For a micromanager, this is the worst thing; they'd rather keep the team stagnant than to let them grow and lose control.

Solution: They must remember that there is a hierarchy in every department for a reason. They need to rely on the team that they hired to do specific work. Not adhering to the organization's hierarchy will diminish the entire team's capacity to grow, including themselves. The problem is that this is an acceptable outcome for them as long as they maintain control. You need to continually remind them that you were hired for a reason, and they should let you do your job. They should focus on reviewing results; not every step that was taken to achieve those results.

SIGN 6: THEY SECOND-GUESS DELEGATING WORK OR JUST CAN'T DELEGATE COMPLETELY...

You often hear a true micro-manager say something like, "By the time I show them how to do it, I could've done it myself, twice." Or "Why should I waste time training them to do it, I'll just have to fix the whole thing anyway." The problem with this thinking is that by the second or third time the employee performs the task, the time spent training the employee has been gained back by the manager. Now for the foreseeable future, he has reclaimed that time. There are legitimate circumstances where time is of the essence. And showing someone else how to do something that is needed immediately might not be the best solution. If your manager can't seem to delegate things that he shouldn't be doing in the first place, he is probably a micro-manager, that can't delegate. Or worse, he decides to try delegating but then immediately second-guesses his decision and regrets it – total nightmare.

Example: Periodically, businesses will send their managers out for training or a management conference. Somewhere in that training is a class or two about managing people or becoming a more efficient manager, something like that. What tends to happen is the manager comes back from the training all gung-ho. Something clicked, they had an epiphany, and they are hell-bent on making some changes. One of the changes you may encounter is the need for the manager to delegate work (that he shouldn't be doing in the first place). They probably just learned that in order to actually get their work done (the work they SHOULD be focusing on), they need to delegate the work they shouldn't be doing. You usually run into this problem when someone gets promoted. Micro-managers that have been performing tasks for a long time tend to have a hard time giving those tasks to someone else. They tend to have one of the two philosophies outlined above. (I can do it quicker than I can show them, or I'll have to fix it anyway.) Instead of trying to delegate their old responsibilities, so they can focus on their new jobs.

You have been elected to take on a new project (one of your manager's old projects). You receive some training, and you are let loose to complete the task. In your opinion, the job isn't that difficult. You may have a question or two, but you took notes, and you don't see this project as anything more than an extension of your new duties. Unfortunately, your gung-ho, micro-managing boss starts thinking about the project. They start second-guessing everything. Did they show you how to do this, or how will I review it if he doesn't do it exactly as I did it? Even silly shit that nobody should spend a second of time worrying about like, what if they use a different font or color? He eventually starts second-guessing the whole delegation process. They start thinking things like, "That class from the manager's conference might work at a big corporation but not at our little company" (or vice versa depending on where you work).

This rationale will be your undoing. I don't say that lightly. Because at this moment, your micro-managing boss starts to freak out. The project that they've been completing for X number of years is being done by someone else. They start thinking, "I must check it and see what they are doing…" Usually, at this point, meetings upon meetings may ensue to go over every single number in the project. They question every single formula. They question any format change. If you improved the process by using technology to automate something, they would need to know why it's not exactly the same as their method. (I found this happened a lot when I used pivot tables to summarize data instead of typing hundreds of numbers into a spreadsheet in the "right format.") How do they know the pivot table is correct? (Trust me, it's more accurate then keying hundreds of numbers into a spreadsheet.)

I finally got myself out of his office, so he could complete the review process without me sitting there. I stepped out for lunch, and on my return, I see the report printed out sitting on my desk with literally fifty lines, x's, and notes throughout the entire report. The funny thing was there wasn't anything wrong with any of the numbers. The report told the same story it always told, but he couldn't understand why I did things differently. He couldn't understand the format change, and this freaked him out. He had lines and circles around titles and headings, telling me what font to use and exactly what size to make everything. He wanted to go back to his format. He probably spent an hour and a half writing on this four-page report all of the ridiculous (and insignificant) changes. In his mind, the way he prepared and presented it was the best, any other way would be inferior to his approach.

So I made changes (the format changes only took a few minutes to fix), and later in the day, I went into his office to discuss the report. Now even with the high multiple, I set for this project. (it was the first time I did it, so I set the multiple at about 2x or 2.5x). I knew that by using technology instead of manually transferring hundreds of numbers from a printed report to an excel spreadsheet would save me a lot of time over his old manual process. I was 100% ready to explain this to him. He goes, "Close the door," and I comply, I close the door and sit down. Then he turned in his chair and grabbed a few sheets of paper from his printer. He laid out the report on his desk and said, "Now this is how this f*cking report should look. This is why I can't trust anyone to do my job" He re-did the whole report. WOW. Now that is a micro-manager.

Solution: Well, I never fully resolved this issue with that manager. I left that department a few months later (Luckily, this company had an excellent internal job-posting system, and they encouraged people to post for open positions within the company). He was an extreme case, and it was very apparent that I had no chance of growing my career working for him. The proper solution would be to try and reason with the micro-manager. Sometimes if you explain why you are doing something different (e.g., it saves a lot of time or using automation eliminates most human error), they can reason it out in their mind. It may take them a little while, the thought has to linger in their brains for a few days or over the weekend, but most people will come around. As far as changing the fonts or colors goes, this is so immaterial to the overall project, I'd use this as a compromise.

Just change the fonts or heading sizes and sell them on the idea of using a more automated approach to completing the project. (Remember more automation equals a larger multiple.)

The second solution is to talk to your manager about trust. When he got promoted, someone trusted him to take on new and more complex responsibilities. Now he needs to believe that you can do the job that you were hired (or promoted) to do. Again, this might take a little while to sink in, but if you consistently prove to be trustworthy, (hopefully) he should come around and start to let go, delegate and trust you.

SIGN 7: THEY LOVE DETAILS AND REPORTS, AND DETAILED REPORTS. A NEVER-ENDING AMOUNT OF DETAILED REPORTS

Does your manager love to see data, details, and reports? Lots and lots of data, details, and reports? Micro-managers tend to think that having more data and details and presenting all of this detail is always a good thing. The one thing they fail to realize is that most non-micro-managers do not need to see every aspect of every transaction, stratified in every possible way. There are those beneficial reports, and then there are those that only exist to show the company, "Look at how much work we do in this department." The problem is that a micro-manager can't distinguish between the two.

Have you ever worked at a company and things are going smooth? Your monthly analysis reporting goes out like clockwork, and people use the detailed reports that you send.

People take action and either fix things or get back to you with explanations right away. Every process that you've designed is running efficiently, and nobody in the organization requires more complex analysis. Things are going so smooth that you've shortened the time it takes you to compile your monthly analysis and send it to the stakeholders in the organization. You think things would be great for all involved, but after a few months of this, you realize it isn't sitting right with your boss. You get the dreaded **Month-End Reporting** invite on your calendar, and you know the jig is up. For no good reason, your manager needs to change the month-end reporting process completely. Instead of the useful reports that have been distributed to much acclaim in the organization, now he has the idea that we need to breakdown everything six ways to Sunday. You know that he loves super complex, detailed reports, showing every penny in the organization, but honestly, who else is going to look at this info? Maybe he has a new boss, and he's going to show him how much analysis we can produce each month. So all of the efficiencies that we gained in the month-end process are now lost. (It probably will take longer than ever to complete the month-end reporting process.) The funny thing is, I find that most of the added reporting tends to go away over time. It's like my manager just had to show the world how complex we can report the numbers. (But nobody seemed to care.)

Example: It doesn't always have to be an external analysis. I've worked for micro-managers that couldn't get enough data or reports each month. Each month they are fiending for you to finish compiling the data. "Do you have my data?" was a common question I received at the beginning of each month. One CFO I worked with loved reports and analysis. Each month, we'd compile the details for the month, and from that detail, I created a few useable reports for him (using pivot tables). I had one tab with all of the data and then a few tabs containing two or four reports on a tab. He loved this.

But then each month he would stop by my office and say something like, "Can you do a report showing the costs by branch, by discipline, by the line of business?" Then he'd want reports by the line of business, by discipline, by branch, and then he'd want one by... (you get the idea). This report kept growing until it became the monstrosity, which became affectionately known as *"The Dump."* We called it the dump because it because a became a pile of unusable shit. This thing grew to about eighty tabs with about 150-200 different reports. I'd have to drop in the details and then refresh all fifty tabs, and it would take forever. And chances were, he would keep thinking of a new way to look at the data and request new tabs and reports. I'm not sure if the new reports superseded the old reports because he would never let me delete any of the old tabs. There was no way he could have analyzed all of the reports on all of the tabs, but he loved having them. The unfortunate thing was that there was no sign of him slowing down wanting new reports, and Excel was getting to the limit of what would refresh without crashing. I had to try and talk to him.

Solution: I tried to explain to him that he could rearrange the reports if he needed to see them differently. So, instead of having to refresh every report every month, he could create only the reports he needs. Unfortunately, this would have involved training him to use pivot tables, which he has been saying, "I gotta learn how to use pivot tables," for six years. He's probably still saying it ten years later. So the solution we came up with was creating a second dump. Or "Dump Jr." This contained ten or twelve reports that he was using currently. The compromise was not to get rid of the original dump, but because it took over an hour to refresh, I'd only refresh it if he absolutely needed to look at it. Fortunately, he never did.

Sure, the Dump Jr. changed a bit over time, but I was able to keep it to a manageable amount of reports, and when something new came in, I usually swapped something out. I just never told him. I just did it, and thankfully, he never asked.

As far as third party reporting, when your manager decides to take your usual reports and amp up the complexity and volume of the analysis (and you know nobody is really going to spend the time to look at these new reports) you just have to ask him, "What is the purpose of this level of detail?". He'll always come back with something like, "How can people manage if they don't have the data?" (Or something like that). You have to keep pressing him, "Do you really think they are going to spend the time going through all of this data? They barely have time to analyze what we currently send them." You need to get the conversation to the following point, "Let's ask them first before we put all of this time into revising our reporting." Now, if you work for a reasonable manager (a non-micro-manager) or at least only a slight micro-manager, then this will seem like a logical step to take before making your department spend days updating your reporting into what is essentially *"A Dump."* But if you work for a true micro-manager, then you will probably get a response similar to this: *"BUT I WANT TO SEE IT."*

At that stage, further arguing is pointless. The only thing you can do is increase your multiple, so he thinks it takes you a hell of a long time to finish.

SIGN 8: THEY CONSTANTLY MISS DEADLINES WHEN FINISHING PROJECTS

When I am given a project to complete, whether it's a one-off project or something that becomes part of my monthly routine, I always look at the due date and work backward. This way, I can work in a decent multiple and make sure it gets done on time. Nobody ever questions my multiples when things get done by the due dates. It's the golden rule for a good work-life balance.

Working for a micro-manager, you know there is a pretty good possibility that he will inject himself into the process. The idea of you completing something without his input must drive him mad because instead of working on his work, he is compelled to manage your project. He'll tell you what to do, who and when to send reports and templates to, he'll put calendar meetings on your calendar (and everyone else involved), every time you try to compile data and complete the project, he'll call someone else to get more updated data… Once you do compile the data, he gets fixated on every single penny or every little piece of data (no matter how immaterial it is – we'll spend hours moving $50 here and there, in a 200-million-dollar company). Projects tend to miss their deadlines when your micro-managing boss gets involved. The sad thing is if he wasn't involved from the start, the project (or at least the first draft) would have been done on time. Then he could lock himself in his office and review every penny on the schedule, to his heart's content, without you having to sit there and explain everything – oh, wait – that would be a normal manager, but you work for a raving micro-manager, so forget that idea.

If you work for a micro-manager, then at least some of this must sound familiar.

Example: I've been in charge of the budgeting and planning aspect of the company for the good part of a decade. I send schedules with historical trends to various departments and ask them to help me compile the piece of the budget that relates to their department. At our quarterly management meeting, in our presentation for upcoming events, my manager explained that this was budget time and that I **OWNED** the budget process (and I have for years). We gave deadlines for the budget, and I explained that I would be recruiting their teams to help achieve this goal. This was nothing new; everyone in the room was aware that this process happened at a specific time of the year. I knew right away that left to my own devices, I would easily hit the deadline and produce a complete budget (at least a complete, compiled first draft of the budget). But I knew, from experience, that these deadlines would mean nothing once my micromanaging boss got involved.

It didn't take long for him to consume himself in the budget process. Instead of me managing the process that I supposedly "owned," my manager is sending emails to every department, telling me to send out templates and trends, like the warning sign above, he needs to be cc'd on every email. Look, I work at the company by choice (any company that pays pretty good and allows me to use a high multiple is appealing to me) so I can always leave if this bothers me (and believe me, I've thought about it – trust me). I know going in that this is going to happen. It always happens. Remember, I work for a raving micromanager. But I also know that as soon as the proverbial shit hits the fan and my boss starts getting involved doing my job, that all bets are off when it comes to deadlines.

If I had a month to complete a draft of the budget, I would send out the templates, as he mentioned. I would schedule calls to discuss anything that warranted a discussion; he needs a face to face meeting, and all departments in my company work at different locations, some in different states, so face to face meetings are more difficult and time-consuming to schedule. I would take the information provided and compile the first draft so we can see how things look without getting into the weeds on every single penny, right away. He would instead meet and continuously go back and forth, knit picking $20 here and $100 there. He'd rather go through every minuscule detail before compiling the data and seeing the big picture.

And we miss the deadline.

I don't care because it's an artificially created deadline that my boss concocted. There are no repercussions if we are a week late on finishing. But inevitably, he will stop into my office and say something like, "You know you're late on the budget" or "You blew the deadline on the budget," I missed the deadline. Now I could do some knit picking myself and point out all the reasons that his meddling made me miss the budget deadline. But that won't do any good, in true micro-managing format, he won't hear you or acknowledge anything you say. In his mind, if he didn't step in and manage the process, this never would have gotten done (remember they don't like delegating or giving credit, and as we'll see later, they always have the best solution for every situation.)

The funny thing is, they don't only hold up your work, but they hold up everyone else's work also. By always having to go back and meet with people about the project and question people about their department's work, they cause company-wide delays across the board. So even though you only really see your side of the story, when you speak to other people, in other departments, they tend to have the same frustrations as you are having. They have their work to complete, so having to have four meetings instead of just one will cause delays for them (just like it's causing you to miss your deadlines.)

Solutions: As far as other departments are concerned, they should go to their managers and tell them that your boss is causing them massive delays (at least after the first couple of meetings and requests for information). If your boss is affecting their department, then their manager should be able to get your boss to back off. Maybe he can ask them questions once a week instead of randomly.

But where does that leave you?

One solution to this problem is to tell your boss that you have scheduled a time to compile the first draft. "I scheduled tomorrow afternoon to compile the first draft." Then document whatever reason he gives you for not compiling the first draft, "No, we still need, updated roster, updated insurance… etc.." At least, you have documented proof that he is the cause of this project not getting done on time. If he gives you the old "You really blew the deadline," you can hit him with facts. "I was going to compile it on the 5th, but you said not to because we needed X, Y and Z. Then on the 10th I started compiling but you told me you were still waiting to discuss that thing with so and so…" Honestly, he'll never admit any wrong-doing. In his mind, he had to step in and get all of these numbers. If he didn't go back and forth with every department, something might have been wrong. Thanks to his "leadership," we now have the right info to compile the report. This logic still doesn't prove how you *"blew the deadline,"* but in his mind, that is exactly how he sees it. Just remember to have everything documented in case this deadline ever comes to disciplinary action. A third party might be more reasonable.

SIGN 9: THEY OVER-INSTRUCT, REMINDING YOU 45 TIMES TO DO SOMETHING, WITH FIVE FOLLOW-UP MEETINGS

Some managers feel the need to give you complex, step-by-step instructions, even for simple tasks. What's most funny about this is that I usually know how to do what he wants better than he knows. So spending half an hour explaining how he wants something done is usually a huge waste of time. This is where you might experience it taking longer explaining something than actually doing the work. But, sometimes, the time spent explaining precisely how he wants something done is completely justified. It's a beneficial meeting when you have questions about the task, and you and your manager work through the details together. That's how it is with a normal manager, but for a micro-manager…

During the project, they "check-in" with you to see how you are "making-out" with the project. For a large project that took a couple of weeks to complete, I had about 45 of these "check-ins" (I'm only slightly exaggerating). It seems that every two hours, I was getting a call, or he stopped by my office, or I received an email or even an instant message. (I'm surprised he didn't start texting me). He just needed to know "the status."

Every time "the status" hit a milestone, he would want to sit down and go over it. He'd need me to walk me through everything I did to that point so that he could review the work. (Even though having only a partially completed project probably caused more questions than answers, he couldn't wait for me to finish.) The advantage here is that with each review session, there were more and more questions and changes, which led to more questions. So every time we sat down and "went over" the project, my multiple grew a little bit. Now I have a reason to miss a deadline. He will never admit that his meddling caused you to miss a deadline, but I have everything documented (in case a missed deadline ever causes disciplinary action). He sends out follow-up emails outlining everything we just went over, so he documented everything for me. (Most micro-managers are good at this type of stuff.) Just an FYI – to date, I've never been disciplined over missing a deadline. Honestly, the only deadlines I miss are for projects that my manager injected himself (unnecessarily) into, and he is well aware of the missed deadline. (Which is 100% his fault, but he'd never admit that.)

SIGN 10: IT'S THEIR WAY OR THE STAIRWAY. THEY HAVE THE BEST APPROACH FOR EVERY TASK

"If you want something done correctly, you must do it yourself." I have no doubt a raving micro-manager wrote this saying. But that is the mentality of the micro-manager. They will waste time doing something I if they think that you cannot do it the same way that they do it. This goes back to their problem delegating work. They have a real problem seeing new ways to accomplish tasks or projects. This is especially true when someone gets a promotion, and you are hired to fill their old position. They have been doing project X for ten years; the exact way they compile it always worked for them, so any deviation cannot be correct. And why would you want to change the way

it's been done for ten years? (Picture the guy who uses Lotus 123 instead of Excel or the real old school guys who still use a pencil and ledger paper instead of ANY spreadsheet.) I'm not saying you need to change something for the sake of change, but if there is a better way, (newer technology, or a more efficient way to do something – maybe using pivot tables to summarize data instead of manually keying numbers on a spreadsheet) we should evolve to the better way.

This also shows that the manager has little faith in you and the other members of the department. Remember, he hired you for a reason, maybe because he isn't tech-savvy or maybe because of your prior experience. Either way, you bring a new dynamic to the table, and a good manager should, at least, hear you out to see if your way is a better way. (They might still overrule you, but they should let you make your case.) The problem I find with non-tech managers, they are scared because if you change the way something is done, using a more technological method, they might not understand what you did, and they might not understand how to review your work. If this is the case, your best bet would be to prepare the work, explain to him why it's better, and walk him through step-by-step how you accomplished it. Sometimes you need to get them comfortable with the method you are using. If they didn't know something like pivot tables existed, they might be blown away by the simplicity and power that pivot tables offer, but until your manager sees step-by-step how to create one, they might be intimidated by the idea of pivot tables.

Sometimes you have to train them to trust you.

SIGN 11: THEY DO MOST OF THE TALKING AT DEPARTMENT MEETINGS

I hold weekly meetings with the department heads in my group. One aspect of these meetings is to see what everyone is working on in the upcoming week. We brainstorm ideas to see if other departments within my group can help or at least share some thoughts about how to accomplish the team's goals as efficiently as possible. Another thing we do at this meeting is to see what challenges each group is facing, and we try and collectively come up with the best solution. This accomplishes a couple of things; one of the other groups may have some excellent ideas about how to solve the problem. Maybe they have dealt with a similar circumstance, or perhaps they know the computer system a little better, or they can spare a few hours and help them. The other thing this accomplishes is just making the other groups on the team aware that something is happening. Maybe we are undergoing an audit, and one group is tied-up gathering information, or this week is another department's busy part of the month. So everyone is aware, and if they cannot help, at least they know to try not to bother that group this week. It just gives visibility to what everyone in the department has on their agenda the following week.

The thing I love about the departmental meeting is the collaboration of ideas and thoughts, it helps us solve problems, but it also brings us together as a group. The meeting helps when I hire a new manager in my department. It's a great way to get them acclimated to the rest of the team. It helps create that bond and also lets them see what everyone else is working on.

On some occasions, my manager sits in on the meeting. When he attends the meetings, the whole atmosphere changes. Instead of a collaboration of ideas, he rambles on about what he wants to happen in the department. I'm not saying he shouldn't mention things that need to be accomplished in the department meeting, but I wanted to point out that the whole purpose of the meeting changes. When people do try and speak, he continuously cuts them off. Or if he wants to say something while someone else is speaking, he will keep repeating the beginning of the sentence until the other person stops talking and lets him continue.

He'll start to say something continuously like, "But," when another person is talking. "But we," the other person tries to finish what they are saying. "But we," other person gets cut off again and tries quickly to finish their thought. "But, but, but, but… (until the other person stops talking all together) But we need to get this done by…" Then he'll apologize for cutting the person off. "But, but, but, sorry, but we need to…" Is he sorry? I say no, because the next time he needs to say something, he'll do the same thing again.

It's irksome. People start to feel like their contributions aren't being considered or valued. That is not the purpose of my department meeting. He could draft an email with bullet points, telling the group what he needs to be accomplished. It would be more efficient and would let the employees retain their collaborative status during the meetings.

SIGN 12: THEIR TEAM HAS CONSISTENTLY HIGH TURNOVER

If you're noticing an alarming trend, losing seemingly good employees after a year or two, this can be a tell-tale sign of a micro-manager problem. The funny thing is good employees don't enjoy being micro-managed. They are good because they can work independently. You can give them some direction, and they can take the reins and run with it. They tend to be able to manage people effectively because they know what they're doing, so people look to them for guidance. A good employee needs minimal handholding. But it seems to be the case that a true micro-manager will feel more compelled to manage every aspect of the employee's day. I don't know if it's because they don't want to be out of the loop, or they want to make sure they understand everything that's being done, but the micro-manager constantly watches over everything everybody does. They interrupt the daily flow by having regular impromptu meetings to go over every detail of a project. I think what it comes down to is control. They need to be (or at least feel) like they're in control at all times. Unfortunately, they assert their control over the people who probably don't need to be controlled, and this causes companies to lose a lot of talented people much sooner than they should. Even if the employees don't quit or transfer right away, being controlled tends to cause resentment, a lack of enthusiasm, and ultimately, employees become much less productive.

On the flip side, people who come in to punch a clock, do the work, and leave don't mind being told what to do. They would probably feel weird if they weren't being told exactly what to do. These employees aren't necessarily bad, but they aren't the superstar employees that you'd promote to take over your position when you get promoted. What tends to happen is these clock punchers tend to stay because it's what they think a job is, I punch-in, and I'm told what to do, and then I leave at a particular hour. So over time, the department with the micro-manager collects more and more of these clock-watchers and loses more good talent. Sure, the manager has total control of the department, but it gets harder and harder for him to move ahead because most of the talented people end up leaving the department before anyone gets promoted.

A lot of companies will try and do fun things to add to the morale of the workspace. They will get food for employees, take them bowling, buy a pinball machine for the office. Most companies don't want to admit that it's the manager's fault for the high turnover. The senior management of the company promoted the micro-manager in the first place, so it's a lot easier bringing in a Pac-Man machine than admitting they were wrong. Some companies will objectively look at the statistics and question why manager A lost 20% of his people, while manager B kept 94% of hers. They will dig deeper and hopefully try to get some training for the managers, so they learn how to manage more effectively. But this is wishful thinking in most cases, or it could take years before the company realizes the problem. They usually realize it when they start to analyze the cost of high turnover. It costs a company a lot of money to replace an employee, and it costs even more to replace a good employee. There's the cost of rehiring, training the new employee, lost productivity, potential work gaps (if someone leaves before you can hire a suitable replacement), plus if you are replacing an excellent employee you may have to go through a few people before you find a suitable alternative (an interview only tells so much).

You probably spend more time at work than with your friends and spouse combined. If you hate going to work, then your whole life will start to suck. One thing that can cause a person to absolutely dread going to work in the morning is a micro-managing boss. A micro-manager makes it almost impossible for you to grow in your career because they constantly are involved with every little detail of every project that you are working on; they smother you. It's like if you put something over a fire so that it gets no oxygen, the fire goes out. It was smothered. That is the best analogy I can make to explain how your career with be stifled, working for a micro-managing boss. As I said earlier, if this is your dream job and there is nothing like it anywhere near your home, then remain working for the company. Always remember to use all of the tactics in the first chapters. The multiple, the list, this way, you can start to control the micro-manager to some extent. If there are plenty of opportunities, whether at another company in your general vicinity or at your current company (a lot of companies post job openings), then always be on the lookout for a better opportunity. One that will help you achieve your goals (e.g., working for a very supportive manager who will help you grow in your career rather than smothering you). Most companies make you stay in a position for a certain amount of time before you can apply for different job openings within the company. In that case, see above, use the multiple, the list, and every other Office Sleuthing technique you learn from this book to get past the minimum timeframe that you need to stay in your current position.

I've outlined twelve common traits of a micro-manager. This is by no means a complete list, but this should give you a pretty good idea of how micro-managers tend to act in the office. I can only assume what they are thinking, but I feel it ultimately comes down to control. They need to be in control of every situation. Whether it's control of a process, or control of a person, they need to be knee-deep in the weeds instead of looking at the big picture. It's the difference between being a manager and a leader. (We'll look at what makes a great leader in the next chapter.)

CHAPTER 8 – MANAGERS VS LEADERS

Now that we can identify what a micro-manager looks like, and I think we can all agree that it's not in your best interest to work for a raving micro-manager, so I'd like to talk a bit about leaders. More specifically, what does a leader looks like compared to a manager (not necessarily a micro-manager). What does someone who manages a process look like compared to someone who leads?

Not all managers are micro-managers. I want you to understand that. The last chapter spent a decent amount of time going over the warning signs of a micro-manager, but some people who manage are much more effective as managers than a typical micro-manager. Some people are just excellent managers, and there is nothing wrong with that. But when you are thinking about the best position for your career, I want you to know the difference between a manager and a leader. I think you will see by the end of this chapter that if your goal is to grow and move up the ranks of an organization, it's in your best interest to work for (or work with, as you'll soon see) a true leader.

TELLING VS COLLABORATING WITH YOU

A typical meeting with a manager to go over a new project might sound something like this:

"We have this new project that our department needs to get by Oct xx. The overall gist of the project is this... Ok, Mark you will do this Friday, and send it to me. Sarah, you will do this by Thursday and then send it to Mark on Friday so he can add to his thing before sending it over to me. Joe, do this, Mary, do that... I will collect all of your work and compile it into the big report that the company needs by Oct. xx. Any questions? Ok, good. Let's get to work."

A typical meeting with a leader to go over a new project might sound something like this:

"I have some great news for our department. We were chosen to do this project for the company. I know we will do an amazing job putting this together and make this incredibly useful for the management team to digest and immediately take action. Here is the description of what they're looking for (reads description). So, let's go around the room and see what everyone is thinking. I know if we work together on this, we will exceed their expectations. (People start to give suggestions) Mary, that is an excellent idea. Ok, if we do that thing that Mary just said and then added the analysis, Dan just mentioned I think we would be off to an excellent start. Listen, the company is counting on us. My door is always open. Remember, no idea is a bad idea. Even if it is a bad idea, I still want the group to hear it because maybe we can tweak it to make it an excellent idea. Ok, Mary, Dan, start putting those ideas to paper. Let's all give this some thought and regroup at 4 o'clock and see if we can flesh this out further. This opportunity is very exciting. We will do great if we work together as a team."

Do you see the difference? The manager is doing what he knows, managing (he is not a micro-manager), but he is managing the project, nevertheless. The manager tells his people what to do. He tells them when to do it, and where to send it once it's complete. The manager doesn't consider the employee's ideas. I'm sure if an employee made a valid point, the manager would listen and work it into his plan, but, for the most part, the manager is planning every detail, telling everyone what they should do and trust me, will take credit for everything.

Contrast this with a leader. A leader guides the team to achieve something better than one person could create. They guide the team in the direction that they need the team to go, but they don't plan every aspect of a project and then delegate (like a manager does). A leader gets his team to embrace an idea, so rather than giving employees work to do, the employees collaborate on a plan to make something great together. A leader uses the various talents of each employee for ideas and allows them to work jointly on activities rather than only using their expertise for the processing of work. You've heard the expression two heads are better than one, well a leader might use ten heads.

So next time you are in a meeting with your manager discussing an upcoming project, listen to how they describe the project and how they delegate the work. Offer up suggestions and see how they receive them. If you work for a manager, you could try to get the team collaborating on ideas with the manager present. He may be receptive, or he may not. If you do take the initiative, then I think that only benefits you and your career, because you are acting as the leader in this scenario. Some managers will welcome this because it takes a little pressure off of them, but other managers will feel like they are losing control. I think it's worth trying, but you have to play it by ear and see how your manager reacts.

OBJECTIVES AND EXPECTATIONS VS A NEW VISION

A manager tends to focus on concrete objectives, the bottom line, or let's get steps X, Y, and Z completed by Friday. They follow a stricter guideline when it comes to rules because rules are rules. They have a hard time thinking outside of the box. It's funny, on a self-evaluation I did for one company that I worked, I put thinking outside of the box as one of my strengths. My manager (and he was clearly a manager) looked me straight in the eyes and said, "Thinking outside the box, I never understand what people mean when they say that." If you hear this or anything resembling discouragement to see things differently, then you definitely work for a manager. Managers stick to the plan. They often document every step of the project, sometimes they use flowcharts or something similar. Deviation from the procedure is not encouraged. The problem with this way of thinking, the "If it's not broke, don't fix it" mentality, is that, while it's true things usually work out and get finished, things never seem to improve. Processes stay the same, employees don't grow and have harder times getting to the next level of their careers, and the business tends to remain status quo rather than branching off in new and exciting directions.

A leader tends to focus on a vision. Instead of seeing the company as processes and the bottom line, they look to the future. They have an idea for what direction the company is heading and unless they see a reason to think otherwise, they steer the company in that direction. Leaders are much more open to new suggestions from employees, why would they continue to follow the status quo when there is a better idea for how things should get done, and a better procedure for getting the company moving towards their vision. Unlike a manager who dictates instructions to their employees, a leader will encourage their employees to think of better ways to get things done or to think more creatively than in the past. They want to find solutions to achieve their vision, and sometimes the current procedures won't quite get them there.

Let's pretend that Steve Jobs was just a good manager. He would have been content making the Apple II computer, as long as the bottom line was profitable. Maybe now we'd have the Apple XXXII computer with modern components, but we wouldn't have the Mac, the iPod, the iPhone, the iPad, Apple Watch… For these products to come to market, the leader needed a vision, way ahead of time, to develop, market, and roll out to the customers. Not only did they need the vision, but they needed a leader who would stay the course. Sure, some things didn't work out for Apple, but that doesn't stop a true leader. The alternative would be one of the myriads of computer makers of the 80s-2000s. Either they were run, with no clear vision beyond selling computers, and went out of business or were acquired by other computer manufacturers that had more of a vision for their company.

ASSIGNS TASKS VS MOTIVATING AND ENCOURAGING

A manager is in the business of assigning tasks to their employees. He needs you to accomplish these five goals this week by 10:00 am Friday. Stick to the procedures laid out, probably in a procedural manual where they require every employee to document every step taken to achieve a task. If your manager needs every task you perform documented in a desktop manual, published on the network for all to see, then you work for a manager, possibly a micro-manager. While I like the idea of having the procedures documented, in case you are out of the office, I don't like the idea that they can use this against you. (Usually, when it comes to the multiple, I assign to every task). So I usually give a complete bullet point outline of what I do, so someone can do the ten steps necessary to complete the task but this also leaves a lot of room for "other stuff" (or things that make up my multiple), usually something like, I go back and analyze X, Y and Z before submitting the job. These omissions sometimes lead to a conversation with the manager.

Manager: "Then why isn't it documented???" (Just an observation, I read the three question marks in a row as WTF, they want to know.) I just come back with the most logical answer, "I just started doing that and haven't had a chance to update my desktop manual. It's been hella busy with that new…".

Leaders, on the other hand, tend to encourage new ideas and new ways of thinking. Sure they probably want to hear your thoughts to make sure they fit into the leader's vision but once you get the green light you are motivated to continue "thinking outside the box" and using your ideas that will move closer to the vision they have for the company (or department, project, report, whatever). A good leader will get your team working together and collaborate on ideas, after hearing the thoughts from the group, they will foster those ideas with the one goal in mind.

For the leader, the most important thing is the outcome, the goal, the vision. They allow employees to create and grow new ideas. They will buck the system if it leads to achieving a goal towards their vision for the company.

For most managers, the most important outcome is the procedures everyone follows, the bottom line, the deadline (sometimes artificial), the tasks involved (what duties did I assign everyone, let me meet with them every day and make sure they are doing what I said). They usually do not "think outside the box." They would rather stick to the rules of the company, instead of allowing their employee's freedom to collaborate and grow their ideas. They would rather follow the flow chart, like a map, with no deviation (also with no improvement).

CONTROL VS TRUST

As we've identified in the last chapter, micro-managers are all about control. They need to control the process, control the situation; they try and control every aspect on which you work each day. But even if your manager isn't a micro-manager, a manager, by very definition, needs to control. Dictionary.com defines a manager as "a person who has control or direction of an institution, business, etc., or of a part, division, or phase of it" also "a person who controls and manipulates resources and expenditures, as of a household." By definition, control is in a manager's job description. So we get back to a manager who needs to control the project. Every aspect, every step, every process typically comes from the manager, "their plan." The staff isn't trusted to accomplish even basic tasks. So, these tasks are all reviewed by the manager. Discipline may result if an employee deviates from the plan.

Let's contrast this with the Dictionary.com definition of a leader, "a person or thing that leads" or "a guiding or directing head, as of an army, movement, or political group." Now, a person that leads isn't the ideal definition; it's the type of explanation that would make most people say, "no kidding." It's obvious that a leader, leads just like we can say a manager, manages, but the interesting definition is the second definition — a guiding head. Notice a leader doesn't control, by very definition, a leader guides their employees (this is why people will follow a great leader). A good leader will trust their team, and the people on the team for a reason. A leader will present his or her vision and allow the team to recommend ideas for accomplishing that vision. Once the ideas are fleshed out, the team usually runs with each of their pieces. They collaborate when necessary. Until the group needs to meet again to see how the project is coming along. Then, the leader will need to guide the team in the right direction to keep them on course with the overall objective. A leader trusts their team. They should only put a team together that they can trust. A leader should have an open-door policy and help people by guiding them through any questions that they have without the need to control everything a person does.

I think it's safe to say that to grow and advance your career, you will be best served by seeking out and working with a great leader. A leader will make you part of the team, a team where your opinions matter, procedures can be improved, and where you can make a real difference in the organization. A leader will give you credit for your accomplishments. Conversely, I view a manager as a follower. They follow procedures and processes, step by step, without giving much thought to improvement. It's the old "if it's not broken, don't fix it," mentality. Instead of being part of a team that can make a real difference, you are on the manager's team. He or she will tell you what to do, how to do it, and review your work to make sure you haven't deviated from their plan. A manager is less likely to give you credit for your work and accomplishments, mainly because they see the entire project as their idea; you were just a part of completing it.

Not all managers will do everything I mentioned in the chapter. There are varying levels of managers. There is less trust. Usually, new managers and ones with low self-confidence will be more extreme (even to the point of being micro-managers), while some managers are much closer to being true leaders. You have to play it by ear when evaluating the groups (or teams) you are assigned, if you find yourself saying more often "the person I work for" rather than "the person I work with" you probably work for a manager. Managers are followers. I believe strongly that you should try to never work for a follower. By following a follower, you can only go as far as one step behind what your manager is capable of accomplishing, following a leader allows you to pave the way for bigger and better things.

In the next chapter, we'll discuss the all-important self-evaluation and how you can nail this one bigly.

CHAPTER 9 – ACING THE SELF REVIEW

In most companies, you get an annual review. The review either happens on your anniversary date (the date you first started working for the company), or everyone in the company gets reviews annually at the same time. For our purpose, it doesn't matter except that your raise will probably be prorated your first year if they review everyone on the same date.

For example, you start working at the company on April 30. If they review everyone on their anniversary date, then every April 30, you will get reviewed (and if April 30 slips into May, remember to ask for your raise retroactive from April 30. – it's a little trick some companies use not to pay a few weeks of a raise – although most will pay you retro without an issue, you may have to ask for it.) The other option a lot of companies use is reviewing the whole company on a specific date. Say they want to wait until the audited financials are issued so they know the profitability of the company for the year (this is usually the case when calculating and paying out bonuses). In this example, the company has an annual review for all employees on June 30. So year one, you technically should get reviewed on June 30, and they would prorate any raise earned for two months (your start date of April 30 to June 30.) The increase should be your total annual raise x 2/12. I said that you should technically get reviewed because most companies are not going to give you a review and a raise after two months. It's just too early in most cases to properly evaluate your accomplishments and assess a realistic increase in salary. This is where our self-evaluation plan will help you pick up those extra two months of prorated compensation. I know we haven't talked about the self-evaluations yet but remember that if they pass you over on the first June 30 review (and they probably will), make sure you get those extra two months included in your next annual review.

WHAT IS A SELF-EVALUATION AND WHY DOES IT MATTER?

To get reviewed (and a nice fat raise) at most companies, you have to perform a self-evaluation. It would be hard for most managers to keep track of every one of your accomplishments for the year – they should be tracking their achievements or the achievements of the team as a whole. So somewhere around a month before your scheduled annual review, you get an email from Human Resources with a template attached asking you to complete a self-evaluation. If your company required a self-evaluation, then you won't get an annual review until you complete it. So we better not screw this up!

Most people get this email and then panic. Now they scramble and try to remember everything that happened over the past year and try to jot it down on the self-evaluation. This is problematic for many reasons, but the obvious ones are forgetting things that you've accomplished and not having enough time to complete a polished self-evaluation. Having to scramble to complete a self-evaluation at the end of the year usually takes people a lot longer than it should, and the quality of the self-evaluation isn't as good as it could be. This is pretty much the exact opposite of the Office Sleuth mentality. We strive to do less work while being more productive. With a little planning, we can even make the self-evaluation process a painless and very profitable experience.

I view the self-evaluation like a massive sales pitch. This document is my agent that is working hard to get me the most amount of money (think Jerry Maguire – Help Me, Help You.) This is the one time of the year where get to toot your own horn. This is the sales page on a website. This is where you have to sell the shit out of everything you've done over the past year. Between the self-evaluation and the actual review, you can add thousands of dollars to your income in just a few minutes. Outside of the interview process, it can be some of the most lucrative time you spend all year. (A good self-evaluation and review can turn into several thousand dollars just like a good interview and salary negotiation when you first get hired by the company.)

Now unlike the majority of people who scramble to put anything down on the self-evaluation and will be happy with almost any raise they get, we will have a plan to make the absolute most out of this process and make the case as to why we deserve more than everyone else. (You won't always get it, but it always helps to make the case.) If you except anything they give you and your manager leaves the review feeling that you are completely satisfied, then you just set the bar for all future salary negotiations at this company (or at least with this manager.) If you are an outstanding employee (The typical Office Sleuth), and your review earns you a less than adequate raise of 2-3%, and you express your feeling of disappointment, they might come back with more money right away (because they really don't want you to quit for the first job that offers you a couple of thousand dollars more) or at the very least, they will come to the table next year ready to play. Managers have wiggle room on the allocation of raises, and once you understand how most companies calculate raises, you will be in a much better bargaining position.

HOW DO MOST COMPANIES DIVVY UP THE RAISES?

Most companies get together in a conference room with the "department heads" (people who manage the departments, usually director level and up). This meeting will have Human Resources and Finance (usually the corporate controller or possibly the CFO, depending on the size of the organization.) This group will often have a name like "Compensation Committee" or something similar. For raises, there is a total company pool – say 3% - of the total payroll for the past year. If the total salaries were ten million dollars, a 3% increase would be $300,000 for the next year. The $300,000 represents the total (maximum) pool allocated for raises. Assuming all is fair, and every department gets a 3% raise (in total). Assume the finance group's total salary expense in the current year was $1,000,000, then they would get $30,000 to allocate in pay raises for next year. Companies don't have to split the allocations evenly, suppose one department loses money, the company might allocate zero dollars, and the department head would have to make a case for any exceptions within the department. (usually, it's the superstar, Office Sleuths.)

In a completely fair world, every department gets the same percentage (3% in this example). So, in the example above, the finance department gets $30,000 of total raises to allocate among the employees of finance. Now, this is where the world doesn't have to be so fair, and it usually isn't. Just because the finance group gets 3% to allocate in raises, it doesn't mean that you're capped at 3%. Albeit some managers take the easy way and give 3% to everyone, but the excellent managers, the ones who want to keep their key people (and keep them happy), will allocate based on merit (or worth to that manager). It's entirely possible for you to get a 5% raise and a few other people in your department only to get 2 or 2.5%. In the end, the total payroll spend for finance will only increase the allocated 3%, but that "right-hand" Office Sleuth ended up with a much more substantial raise than other employees. I've even seen managers forgo a part of their raises to keep the superstars happy in their department. The way I see it, if it weren't for the office superstars then the manager wouldn't be successful anyway (just as a point of information, because I know you are asking this question right now, this is the extremely rare exception to the rule. It doesn't happen often.) Most managers think the operation would shut down if they weren't there making all of the decisions, and they certainly would never value one of their employees greater than them self. Not every manager is a good manager. Keeping your team happy, especially key people, is the sign of a good manager.

Even if he/she is a total nightmare in every other aspect of work (like micromanaging, doesn't know simple arithmetic, drinks heavily and passes out at his/her desk) valuing key employees is one trait I look for in a manager. I can look past a lot of other idiosyncrasies, but someone who doesn't appreciate their key employees is a deal-breaker.

I'll also mention that, unless explicitly spelled out in your employment agreement, bonuses are calculated in very much the same method as raises. The department head usually has a list of all bonus eligible employees in their group, and the compensation committee will allocate a certain amount of money to distribute to that group in the same fashion as the raises were distributed. The manager should allocate the bonuses according to the employee's worth to the organization. Using the same logic, if the total finance budget for bonuses was 5% for all bonus eligible employees, there is nothing written that says you have to get 5%. If you are a superstar, an Office Sleuth, you might wind up with a 10% bonus while the other people in your group get a bonus in the 3-4% range.

So, how do we make sure we are on top of the pay scale when it comes to raises and bonuses? It all starts with the self-evaluation.

DOING A SELF-EVALUATION, THE RIGHT WAY.

As mentioned before, most people scramble to prepare their self-evaluations the week before their review. This is the absolute wrong way to go about preparing a self-evaluation. The correct way to prepare a self-evaluation is to prepare for it all year. So, when that week comes that you get an email asking you to complete a self-evaluation so you can get a review (and raise), the self-evaluation is already done. You have to format it the way they require, but everything else is done.

It all goes back to those two magic words – the list.

The list is our most powerful tool, not only to make sure we have an immediate answer when asked what we're working on that day but also to jot down all of your accomplishments for the day. Any time you work on something that is above your pay grade (e.g., your boss's work), make sure you write a quick note about what you've accomplished. Do this each day, and at the end of the week (on company time, during some of your time, of course), summarize your weekly accomplishments in a Word file or whatever way you are most comfortable. Highlight the things you've done that weren't part of your typical responsibilities. At month-end, create a list of all out of title (new or extra) things that you worked on and any major accomplishments. We will derive a lot of our self-evaluation from this list, so it's essential to do, but don't get overly obsessed with it. Once a month, go through your notes in Word or paper or wherever and add to the list. (Yes, you can make a list in Word, if you'd like. Just use a bulleted list and write everything down. I like using Excel because it's easy to sort, but Word works fine also.)

Your self-evaluation will have two components. One is where you maintain your responsibilities. Nothing slips through the cracks; in fact, things have improved from last year. It's not enough to say I have continued to prepare the monthly report. Talk about how you've developed the monthly statement or expedited it:

The monthly report was prepared in four days, down from five in the previous year. Also, we've added department level analysis to add granularity to the report and see if any departments have fallen behind. To date, only department six seems to be struggling. As shown in the new monthly report analysis.

Do not be afraid to toot your own horn. This evaluation needs to trigger a whole year's worth of memories for your boss. He needs to see why you are so valuable. (And why he can't afford to lose you.) This isn't the time to be modest. He should read through your evaluation and continuously say, "Oh yeah, I forgot about that…".

The second component of the self-evaluation is all the new work you did this year. Whether that work was newly added work that has become part of your responsibilities or working above your job title, taking over for your boss when he goes on vacation or even a sizable one-time project where you were intimately involved. You helped implement and test a whole new ERP system. This shouldn't be happening every year, but make sure you document your involvement this year.

This component of your self-evaluation should highlight the fact that you did a lot of new work, even out of title work, and you not only did this extra work, but you've still performed your normal job functions and also improved them. You want to make sure you spell out that this function is new, or it's something you did that was beyond the scope of your job, all while performed your regular duties:

Successfully prepared and sent the report for the Board of Directors while you were on vacation in Maui, fielded their question while maintaining a four-day month-end close. It was good to communicate with the Board. Now they have another resource within our department where they can reach out for answers.

Try to make the new work you have done sound like it permanently has become your work. In the above example, you worked with the Board of Directors while your boss was on vacation. Even if it's not the case, you made it like this is an ongoing thing. You have effectively raised your status within the department. Unfortunately, this can go two different ways with your manager if the manager is confident and is trying to get promoted. Then this should be exactly what they are looking for in their employees. Someone who can take on more of their role, and they can start to groom you to be their replacement. On the flip side, if your manager is not very confident and feels lucky that they have the role they're currently sitting in, they could potentially start to view you as competition. They may begin to feel threatened by you. Either way, I still think you need to document your accomplishments in the self-evaluation. This document is memorialized in your personnel file. One day your manager may quit or get fired, and you find yourself working for someone else. They will review these documents to see your accomplishments.

The self-evaluation is another reason why updating the list is so important. Make sure you don't forget to update it every week and do not forget to list out everything you do, especially things that are over and above the normal course of business — working on the weekend, working from home at night, staying exceptionally late to finish a large project on time. If your company gives you a formatted document to fill out and there is not enough room to list all of your accomplishments, then, by all means, attach a separate document and on the formatted one provided write "See Attached Document." Do not partially fill out the formatted document because then they might accidentally get rid of the attached document listing all of your other accomplishments. You want to make sure they have to read your attached document and placed it into your permanent file.

Now, the other thing any new manager will want to see is your former manager's review and comments about the work you performed. So, how do we talk a paranoid manager who is not too confident off the ledge, so they review us fairly (and favorably we hope)? The review is coming up in the next chapter. It's the second part of our annual review process, and it can contribute even more to our raise and bonus for the year. So, we better make sure we come prepared for the actual review.

CHAPTER 10 – THE SIT DOWN

After submitting your self-evaluation to the company (usually you'll send it to your boss and Human Resources so they can add it to your personnel file), a good boss should thoroughly review it, write-up his or her notes about your performance in each area of the self-evaluation and then present a review to you in writing. I said, 'a good boss' because often managers feel like their time is too valuable to really go line by line through your self-evaluation and adequately evaluate you. If your boss takes the time to do this, then congratulations, they are not only doing their job but think enough about you to spend the time to do it properly. The other great thing about a manager who spends the time writing up his or her evaluation of your performance is that they most likely spent the time actually to read through your self-evaluation. Trust me; I've worked for people who probably didn't make it past the first paragraph or just skimmed the entire four or five-page document. I didn't spend hours compiling this information to be glossed over by somebody who I depend on for my review and future salary increases at the company. Quickly, you'll need to figure out how much time did they think about and prepare for this review.

Did your manager spend the time assessing your evaluation? Did they provide their own evaluation and give you useable feedback? Or did the review pop up on their calendar fifteen minutes before the scheduled time, and now they are scrambling to put something together that sounds like it took them no more than five minutes to complete.

We'll talk about how to deal with both scenarios, but first, how should you prepare for the review?

PREPARING FOR YOUR REVIEW.

During your review, you can gain thousands of additional dollars per year (and potentially a decent bonus) if you can prove to your manager why you are more deserving than everyone else in your group (the group that reports to your manager). Say you make $50,000 a year, the difference between a 6% raise and a 2% raise is $2,000 (6% = $3,000 raise, 2% = $1,000 raise). Now compound the extra raises over ten years (or even twenty years if you plan to stay at the company for your career.) We know that your manager has a certain pool from which they can give raises, suppose the average is 3%, so some people might get 2% some might get zero while others get 4, 5 or even 6%. If taking the time to prepare a solid self-evaluation and showing up prepared for your performance review can potentially gain you an extra one or two thousand dollars raise than someone not prepared, that will turn into serious money over time. Think about this example, you received an extra $2,000 over someone who is mediocre (and their work might be good, but they didn't put the time in, and they submitted a mediocre self-evaluation). You are going to receive that extra $2,000 **EVERY YEAR** going forward. Plus, all future raises are based on your current salary that year. So that raise will grow each year by the percent your salary increases. It's like compound interest in your paycheck – compound salary. When I said that the work you put into your self-evaluation and review is worth thousands of dollars, so the extra $2,000 you receive this year is literally worth tens of thousands over your career). When my coaching students belly-ache about putting in a few hours of work to prepare for the review, I just remind them that the few hours of work spent now can translate into many tens of thousands of dollars over their careers (so every hour spent now on this review might be worth $10,000 when compounded over your career). So, if it seems like I'm harping on the self-evaluation and review process a little, I am.

Regardless of whether your manager prepares for your review or not, you should always come prepared. You did most of the work already when you developed your self-evaluation. This is why it's so important to write down everything you do each day. Even if it takes five minutes a day, write everything down. Then summarize weekly and even re-summarize monthly. You're building the self-evaluation in advance, plus you are reviewing your accomplishments each week and each month. You'll complete your self-evaluation before the time of the review. Even though you've reviewed your accomplishments multiple times throughout the year and you just thoroughly reviewed them again when compiling your self-evaluation, make sure you take some time before your review and study the evaluation. Go point by point for all of your significant accomplishments for the year. Try to put yourself in your manager's shoes, what questions will he have? What accomplishment might he see differently than you? If you take the time and think about these things in advance, your review should go a lot smoother. View your prep time for your review like it's the final exam for the year, the big test where you need to study. If you treat the review process as a final exam and prepare then, you should be able to make the case exactly why you deserve the 5 or 6% raise, while the average employee gets 2 or 3%. That is our goal in this review.

After taking some time to review your self-evaluation, print out two copies and take them with you into your review. I mentioned that you would either have a manager who takes the review process very seriously and will come into it as prepared as you, or they will feel that this review is nothing more than a formality. Something that the manager has to do. I prefer a prepared manager, but we can also work with the other type.

THE MANAGER, AS PREPARED AS YOU

When I see a manager review my five-page evaluation and then add multiple pages of their own notes, I feel good. Why? This manager is showing me that he carefully reviewed and considered all of my points. These are my accomplishments for the year, so even if he doesn't agree with everything I documented in the evaluation, he acknowledged them and wrote up his notes accordingly. When I say he doesn't agree with my accomplishments, it's not that I didn't accomplish the task, it's that sometimes their perspective on something might not match my viewpoint. For example, in a previous chapter, I mentioned that after dealing with the Board of directors for my manager, I offered to become an additional resource for them. In my perspective, this is an ongoing thing, and I am always available to the Board. My manager may not see it that way, he may view it as a one-off type of assignment, and he is still the point of contact for the Board where all communication must go through him. A difference of perspective (or opinion). Having a different perspective of your work from your manager is perfectly ok. The contrast gives you a valid talking point and the opportunity to make your case. Just because he comes into the review with a difference of opinion, doesn't mean that you cannot win him over to your way of thinking. This is why you've been preparing. When you were putting yourself in your manager's shoes and started to think about his perspective and the way he would view your accomplishments, if you realized that he might have a different opinion about the Board of directors you would have expected his comments on the review and then worked out the talking points ahead of time. It might go something like this:

BOSS MAN: "I NOTICED ONE OF YOUR ACCOMPLISHMENTS WAS BEING A DIRECT LINE OF COMMUNICATION FOR BOARD. I REALIZE YOU COVERED FOR ME WHILE I WAS ON VACATION, BUT I DON'T SEE THAT AS ANYTHING MORE THAN A ONE-TIME THING."

YOU: "I DID ANSWER ALL OF THEIR QUESTIONS WHILE YOU WERE ON VACATION, BUT I ALSO HAVE BEEN IN CONSTANT CONTACT WITH BILL SMITH. HE REGULARLY CALLS ME TO GET SALES NUMBERS FOR HIM. PROBABLY TWICE A MONTH. IT ONLY STARTED AFTER I COVERED FOR YOU DURING YOUR VACATION."

BOSS MAN: "OH? I WAS WONDERING WHY I HAVEN'T HEARD FROM BILL THAT OFTEN. NOW HE ONLY CALLS BEFORE OUR QUARTERLY BOARD MEETING."

YOU: "GLAD, I COULD TAKE THAT OFF YOUR PLATE, BOSS MAN..."

The self-evaluation lets you list all of your accomplishments, and the review enables you to sit down and go over the details with your manager. There are plenty of things you've accomplished during the year, that your manager knows about and forgets (not purposefully, he probably has a lot on his plate). But there is also a ton of stuff that he doesn't know about that he needs to know, to give you the most substantial raise possible. So list everything in your evaluation, but be ready to explain every detail during your review. That is why you need to study beforehand.

This logical conversion about my accomplishments is why I find it easier to deal with a manager who comes prepared for your review. He has already thought about everything you said, given his opinions (in writing), and spends the time talking with you about your accomplishments. If you accomplished something (like the example above), you should be able to walk them through why their opinion doesn't exactly line up with yours and hopefully win them over.

THE MANAGER WHO FORGETS ABOUT THE REVIEW UNTIL THE REMINDER POPS UP FIFTEEN MINUTES PRIOR

I've worked for managers who sent me an email instead of an actual review. It said something like, *"I agree with everything you said in your self-evaluation. I'm giving you the full 3% raise. That is the maximum I can give this year. Keep up the good work."* I'm paraphrasing slightly, but that is the gist of my emailed review.

Let me break down this simple four-sentence email and see what's really going on.

- **"I agree with everything you said in your self-evaluation."** Translation: I glanced over your self-evaluation. Nothing struck me as entirely fabricated, so instead of me giving you the time and attention necessary to review you correctly, I'm just going to agree with whatever you said in your self-evaluation. An email is a complete BS response from a manager. First off, never accept a BS email like this. Always respond that you would like to sit down and have a formal review. You work hard all year, documenting your accomplishments. Your manager should take the time and adequately review you. Plus, as we'll see in the next sentence, there is little wiggle room with salary raises and bonuses when dealing with an email like this.

- *"I'm giving you the full 3% raise."* Translation: I was given a pool of 3% to increase the salaries of my employees, so instead of weighing the merits of each employee, I'm just giving everyone 3%. This makes their life incredibly easy because they don't have to show any favoritism to the employees who deserve it. On the one hand, he is trying to prevent a mutiny in his department, but the good employees might be updating their resumes when they find that they received the same raise as the person who is always lagging in the department. The other possibility is that he viewed the 3% raise pool as the maximum he can give an employee, so when he says that he gave you the maximum, he wasn't lying. Maybe he did undercut the laggard employees, but that leaves a little bit of the raise pool on the table. Perhaps your manager thought he'd get a better review if he only used 2% of the 3% allotted for raises. The bottom line is you will never know unless you sit down with the manager for a proper review and go through your accomplishments and make your case why you deserve more than the 3% allotted to the department.

- **"That is the maximum I can give this year."** Translation: Maybe he thinks that is the maximum the company will allow him to give as a raise to employees this year. Again, you'll never know until you talk it over with him. Either he maxed out raises at 3% (for superstars) and scaled them down for underachievers, or maybe he thinks the company is just giving 3% across the board, and everyone is getting the full 3%. This is the reason you need to sit down and properly review your position, your accomplishments, and future goals (we'll cover goals in the next chapter). One way or another, we need to discuss this apparent 'maximum' raise percent and make our case for deserving a larger slice of the raise/bonus pie than others in our department. On the flip side, after the 2008-2009 recession, businesses were hit hard. There were two years the company I worked gave 0% raises. Believe me; those were fun reviews to do with everyone, zeros across the board (while the president leased a brand-new Range Rover). But with sales down 30%, a portion of the company "downsized," you were happy to keep your job. So, in year three, when we were all given 3%, nobody complained. Sometimes you need to look at the bigger picture. If your company just let 30% of its staff go, I might not complain about a 3% raise, but if the reasons are company-specific (and not a global recession like in 2008), I think I would start updating my resume. Not because of the 3% but because it sounds like the company is in trouble. Bottom line, the maximum raise a manager can give usually has a liberal amount of wiggle room for the right employee. A proper sit-down review is where you get to convince your manager that you are the right employee.

- *"Keep up the good work."* Translation: You do good work, and he knows it. This type of comment is screaming for a better than average raise. Your manager is acknowledging your work but, for some reason, has taken the easy way out when it comes to your review. This "good work" is precisely why you need to sit down and have a proper discussion with your manager. He (or she) owes this to you. So don't feel weird about asking for a review. You should reference the "good work" that is noted in the email and request a time to go over it in detail. Plus, we need to look to our managers for guidance. How else can we get to the next level or learn what is expected of me to get a 6% raise? With a BS email saying, "Keep up the good work," we'll never know what's expected of us to grow (beyond our regular, routine day to day). We'll cover goals in the next chapter, but it's your manager's responsibility to set expectations for your development. Your manager should be letting you know the expectations for your success throughout the year, but this needs to be memorialized at the annual review.

The type of manager who would send an email like this, instead of a review, is usually one of two things. He is either lazy or a coward. Most likely, he is just lazy. He feels he is too busy to waste time on a review and will hope to get by acknowledging your work (self-evaluation) without doing any work of his own. He agrees with your five-page evaluation instead of writing up his assessment.

The other type of manager that would send an emailed review like this is a coward. A lot of people can talk a tough game when they're in a group or on the phone with someone but sitting down and constructively criticizing one of their key players can be difficult for this person. This is why you are getting an impersonal email with no real feedback, just a rah-rah pep talk (keep up the good work) is so useless. He is straight lining the raises so that everyone gets 3%, making sure not to offend anyone. But what he's forgetting is that he is insulting the superstars of the department. By giving the same raise to everyone and making it sound like a company policy, he is hiding from actually rating and evaluating his people. This is just bad management all around. It's incredibly challenging to grow working under someone like this, I'd suggest, if it's a possibility, to explore if your company has other job postings under a good, solid manager that will help you achieve your goals.

Unfortunately, without a proper review, not only is it difficult to get a better raise this year, but you won't know what's required to get that fat raise or promotion next year. This is true working for any manager. If your goal is to average a 6% raise each year, then what is required to accomplish this? This is why you need to make your manager work for you during this process. Your future at the company depends on it. Remember, a couple of percentage points per year can turn into tens (or even hundreds) of thousands of dollars throughout your career. You can't let your manager's laziness or cowardliness get in the way of your goals. The thing about this type of manager is they will never put your needs ahead of their needs. The lazy manager is not going to do a ton of work (on his own) to help you get ahead in your career. A cowardly manager probably doesn't want any competition from you, so keeping you in your place helps him feel more confident in his career. Since they aren't going to do it on their own, we'll have to give them a little nudge. If you feel weird about demanding something from your manager, you have to get over it, at least once a year. We need an official sit-down review where we can make our case for increased raises and bonuses, to talk about our plans, and (most importantly) get feedback about how we are doing in our manager's eyes. We need to find out what we need to do to get that 5-6% raise, a more substantial bonus, and that sweet promotion (if that's what you want). This is why the review (especially with this type of manager) is critical. It's non-optional. So, let's prepare for this.

HOW TO PREPARE FOR THE REVIEW WITH A LAZY MANAGER?

The first thing you need to know is exactly where you stand in the department. If you are one of the top employees that work for this manager, then you have some leverage to ask for more than the average (straight-lined 3%) increase in salary. If you are the top employee, your manager's right-hand man, then you should be better compensated than the average run of the mill employee. Knowing where you stand is essential. Even if your lazy boss hasn't thought of your worth, carefully worded comments during your review might make him seriously consider taking better care of you, his right-hand, superstar.

As you sit down and start to talk, you need to control the conversation. If your manager says something like, "I agree with everything you wrote down...", you need to bring the conservation back to the details of your self-evaluation. You can't let him generalize your entire year's accomplishments in one quick statement. You have to go bullet by bullet, over every point you wrote down, discuss each point and get his buy-in (agreement). Some psychologists say if you nod your head up and down (like nodding to say yes), subconsciously, people will say yes, more often. I'm no psychologist, but some salespeople swear by this technique, so I thought I'd mention it.

As you bring up your accomplishments, you don't want to call out other people in your department directly, but I would call out generalized department deficiencies. Instead of saying, "I work twice as fast as Harry.", say something like, "I get the monthly thing done in three days. It took five days when I first started working in the group." You need your lazy manager to see your worth. You can't just let him off the hook with a quick, generic review. You need to go point by point and convince him exactly why you are the best in the department. Even if he knows it already, just hearing you say it (because now he knows you know) might motivate him to try and keep you in the group. Primarily if you work for a large company that has a lot of internal postings for opportunities, other managers might hear of your accomplishments and might make it worth your while to make a move. The last thing your lazy manager would want to do is lose their right-hand.

If all else fails and your manager listens, agrees, and then says, "My hands are tried, or the raises were already submitted, or this is a company policy....". You realize that you are not getting anything more than the standard 3% this year, your next move must be to find out what is required to get a 6% raise (always try to get double the average). Have your boss spell it out exactly. If he doesn't put it in writing on your review, then follow-up with an email memorializing the entire review, everything that was said, and agreed to by your manager. Then send it to your manager telling him that this is your understanding of his evaluation, and you wanted to make sure there were no misunderstandings. Once he agrees, send a copy to yourself, your manager, and HR, so everything is documented and on the record. Sending it to a third party with his acknowledgment makes it easier to hold him accountable. Funny story, I worked in an accounting department as a controller. The accountants would keep notes of everything that happened in the month. If the CFO told them to do something, or record something, they would document it. So one day he came in and started reading the notes, and something he said (that was probably a little shady) had a note that said, "Per CFO" (only it had his real name), he grabbed the accountant's keyboard and started erasing his name from all of the notes. The last thing he wanted was to have his name lighting up the notes to the financial statements. He didn't want to be held accountable, and he wasn't. He just erased the note. This is why you want to document everything you agreed on during your review and send it to a third party because then he has no choice but to be held accountable. (CYA – Especially when it comes to your money)

THINGS TO DO BEFORE EVERY REVIEW

No matter for whom you're working, whether it's a great, organized manager, who has everyone's best interest in mind, or a lazy manager who wants to get past the review process without having to do any work, you have some homework to do before your actual review. I know you went through all of your accomplishments during the self-evaluation process. You laid out your plan for advancement (if that is your goal) and showed your worth to the manager and the department. The first thing you should do before sitting down with your manager is to review your self-evaluation. Review every point, every reason, essentially why you wrote each point. After every bullet, ask, *"So what?"*. If there isn't a good answer to that question, then consider revising or removing that bullet. Everything needs to be relevant. (And this is true in a self-evaluation, a resume, or just writing an email.) Explain how every point will be beneficial to the manager, the department, and the company. This is how you quantify your worth — showing your value to the organization. The review is a place to sing your praises, to talk yourself up. You want to go over all of your accomplishments for the entire year. Make sure the manager schedules adequate time for your review because you don't want to rush through and miss something.

The first thing you should discuss is all of the goals that you and the manager laid out during last year's review. If you agreed on seven goals to accomplish this year, then go one by one through all seven and explain what you did to achieve those goals. Prior year's goals are a good point of reference to start because your manager should have just read last year's review, so this should be fresh in his mind. Go over every goal, how you achieved it or why you didn't achieve it. Hopefully, if you didn't accomplish something, it was because something out of your control prevented you from reaching that goal. If the reason was, "Oh shit, I forgot about that...", then don't mention that goal during your review. The important thing is to get your manager to agree with your assessment of your accomplishments (and agree with the reason why you couldn't accomplish something).

I'm going to go through the steps you need to take, but your manager will have comments in-between each of these steps. A word of advice, if you disagree with his assessment of how things happened, definitely mention it to him. But the review is not the place to get into a knock-down, dragged-out, screaming match. It's better to disagree on this point tactfully. Companies like both parties to sign the review, and this is where you can document every item where you and your manager disagree. Plus, your comments will now be in the permanent records of the company, a screaming match doesn't accomplish this.

Next, go over all of your goals that you'd like to accomplish in the upcoming year. You and your manager might differ a little, but should be on the same page, overall. The review is also where you need to ask your manager exactly what it takes to achieve your next goal. "How do I get to the next level with the company?" or "How do I get a 6% raise and a bonus next year?". Whatever your goals are, you want your manager to spell out the exact steps necessary for you to achieve those goals.

After all the points have been discussed, accomplishments and failures were agreed upon, and goals have been set for the following year, it comes to the best part of the review — your raise/bonus. Now, if you are expecting a 6% raise but during your review, your boss seemed to downplay your accomplishments or worse took credit for your achievements, then I doubt you are going to get that hefty raise you expected. Maybe you get 3%. Maybe he rounds up, so it works out to 3.5% but not 6%. You might have even discussed this last year, and you tailored your goals to hit the 6% mark. If your boss downplayed your achievements, he is setting you up to receive less, or you might have one of those bosses that "forgets" offering you 6% for accomplishing specific goals. (This is why you MUST put everything discussed in the review in writing before signing it and sending it to HR to file in your permanent file.) What should you do in the event your boss forgets your last review or downplays your accomplishments? One word, recon.

Know the job market. Are you in a hot or cold job market for employees? A hot job market is one where companies can't find good people. Everyone is working, making money, and if a company wants to hire talent, they will have to pay (probably a lot more, then they thought). A cold market for employees is just the opposite, think the recession in 2008-9, companies laid off a large percentage of their staff, a lot of people were looking for work, companies were "right-sizing" to the negative, which means they were reducing headcount instead of hiring. The only hires companies were making were replacement hires, but with massive lay-offs and unemployment skyrocketing, many candidates were fighting over the same, limited positions. Competition drives the price down, so if you were an employee somewhere, you probably were happy to be employed and not worrying too much about a 6% raise. A lot of companies gave no raises for a couple of years. My point here is if you are offered a small raise in a hot market you can be a little more aggressive in your negotiations, but if the market is cold (like in a recession), you might want to take what they are giving and plan your next move when the job market heats up.

Another thing to know as you go into the review is, what is my position worth in the market? You can look up comparable positions in the market that you work (location) and see a range of wages that people earn. These websites are not an exact science, but you can gauge your worth vs. your pay in a general way. If staff accountants in your job market (location) make between $48,000 and $57,000 in your size company and you have been working at the company for three years and only make $47,500, then I think you have a valid argument that you are underpaid. I would bring this up in your review. But you cannot just say it, you need to show proof that staff accountants are making between $48-57k and with three years' experience you should be making at least $52,500, so a $5,000 raise is reasonable (and that would be almost an 11% raise so that would be pretty good for corporate America).

Conversely, if you're a staff accountant making $60,000 in this scenario, then you might want to accept the 3% raise. Because moving to a new company would probably not get you more money unless they hired you at a promotional level (like a senior accountant or accounting supervisor). If you like the company and find yourself in the latter scenario, a better conversation to have during your review would be, how do you get to the next level, and how long before your manager thinks you are ready for a promotion? If he still thinks you are three years away from any promotion, and you meet the requirements of the promotional title on different company's job postings (or internal job postings with another department). You may want to start planning your exit move.

So how exactly do you figure out if a job market is hot and what is your salary range? Online has resources to compare salaries and look at job opportunities (postings); they sometimes list salaries. But I think the best source to go to, that has a finger on the pulse of the job market, is employment agencies (headhunters). They will know if the job market favors job applicants or employers because it's their job to know. They will also be the best source to tell you if you are over or under paid because they place candidates all the time in your job category. So they know that a staff accountant with three years' experience makes about $x.xx. Having a good relationship with a couple of recruiters is always a good thing. As they get to know you and get to know your capabilities, you might get a call out of the blue, with an opportunity that just came up. You may not be searching, but sometimes things happen, and an offer presents itself that you cannot refuse. Do your homework online, but then bounce your thoughts against a trusted recruiter to see if your research lines up with reality.

CHAPTER 11 – GOALS, YOUR FUTURE REALIZED NOW

Goals are part of the self-evaluation and review process, but I wanted to give goal setting its own chapter because it's so important to set goals. There are two types of career goals we need to talk about. The first is the goal-related questions that usually show up on either the self-evaluation or during the actual review. These are the goals that are related to the company. These usually come in the form of "What are your goals (or what would you like to achieve) in the coming year" and "Where do you see yourself in three to five years?". These are important questions on the self-evaluation (or the review), and if you aren't currently working, some form of these questions usually shows up during the interview process, so we need to get this right. The second career goals we need to think about is your actual career goals. These will be different for everybody, and they may or may not line up with the goals that we report on the self-evaluation. In a nutshell, the self-evaluation serves the purpose of keeping us in line with company expectations. While our real goals may differ slightly from the company goals because the company, we currently work for may only be a stepping stone to achieve our true goals (and companies tend to frown upon that), so we need to separate our goals.

GOALS - FOR THE COMPANY

I know that almost everyone wants to say, "In three years, I want to be sitting in your chair," but most managers don't want people gunning for their jobs. I say, most managers because a true leader will see themselves two levels up in three years anyway, so they probably are looking for their replacement. A manager, especially an insecure, micro-manager wants to be in control of the process. If they get promoted one day, then you might get promoted, but they usually don't want to work with people who are too ambitious. They do not want anything getting in the way of their control. Saying you want a promotion in three years is a very realistic goal. If that is your goal, then it should be a part of your personal career goals, but when it comes to an evaluation (or a review), a time when you have to tell the company your goals, you must take into account the recipient of the information. Who is your audience? If your audience consists of Human Resources, then it's probably ok to be a little bold on your goals. Human Resources works with all departments and might be able to align your goals with another department's goals and present you to that department for opportunities. But if you have a sit-down review with an insecure micro-manager and you are their direct report, then you have to be a little more politically savvy. If your manager starts to think about your goals and it dawns on him that your goals threaten his plan and you are a viable candidate to achieve your goals, then that may cause you some problems. Even if he's not aware of it, subconsciously, he might react differently towards you. Maybe he's not outright hostile, but every project he assigns to you will first go through his mind to see if it causes a threat. Perhaps he won't want you working on something for senior management because he wants to limit your access to the senior management team. He may not even realize he's doing it, but if someone feels threatened, their brains react to protect them. Usually, this is where people experience the fight or flight reaction. Unfortunately, he may start to fight you (even if it's subconscious) in almost all decisions, and the most threatened might give in to the flight reaction, but instead of him fleeing, he might show you the door. With an excellent Human Resource department, they'll usually need some proper documentation as to cause of termination, but if someone feels threatened enough, they'll figure something out. Most managers would be crazy to fire their best employees, their Office Sleuth, so this isn't the most likely scenario, but it is a possibility. I've seen it and want to make you aware that it has happened.

Knowing your audience is one of the key components in setting goals and expectations on your company review. Since your direct supervisor will, most likely, be the primary recipient, I think you should cater a lot of your responses to what would make them comfortable (and to let them know it's ok to give you a good-sized raise because your goals and their goals are aligned). Talk about your desire for a promotion, if that is your goal, just not so directly as "I want to have your job next year…". The best place to start tracking your company goals is from your trusted list. I would scan the annual list for all accomplishments achieved when doing your evaluation but also brush-up on all of the upcoming projects that your manager has repeatedly mentioned during the year. The most straightforward goals to talk about are ones that you know are coming in the next year or two. These are projects that are probably on your manager's to-do list. It helps him feel comfortable if your goals align with his expectations. In his mind, his expectations have become your goals.

One goal might be the new computer system that your company is converting to next year. Besides the fact that you are getting a new computer system, write up your ideas for implementation and that you'd like to spearhead the project. Then outline your plan for initiating the project, list steps, list people you want to recruit to help you accomplish the project, whatever resources you'll need. Even if he doesn't let you run with it (we know micro-managers have trouble delegating important tasks), writing up your goal in this way achieves a few purposes

- It lets the manager know that your goals and his goals are aligned (you didn't forget the super-sized project), and you have given some thought on what you'll need to do to achieve the goal.

- It lets Human Resources (and any other department) know that you are very proactive and have, not only, listed a goal, but have worked through the very process of managing and completing the task. You must remember that any self-evaluation, review, or goals written down and submitted to a company become part of your permanent file. Something you write this year might help you land a new position two years from now when Human Resources and another manager (preferably a good manager, or even a leader) reads your goals. If it appears that you can think independently and logically work through a project, a leader may want you on their team in the future. Your primary audience is your manager, but you never know who might become your audience in the future.

- Another reason you want to have your methods and procedures for accomplishing your goal (or a significant project) in your permanent file is good 'ol CYA. Suppose your manager completely disregards everything you say. In his controlling, micro-managing mind, he knows best. He implements the entire new system his own way. Who knows, maybe he felt threatened because you had a great idea on how to achieve the goal, or perhaps he never really considered your idea in the first place. Suppose the manager fails miserably at trying to accomplish the goal. A couple of things could happen:

    - He could try and blame someone else for the failure. In that case, you have documented proof of how you thought he should have handled the project. If he tries to blame you, you're covered (and that is in your permanent file so he shouldn't be able to delete it). This is a document you'll want to have reviewed if any disciplinary action is taken against you for your manager's failures.

- Someone else comes in to fix the problem, finish the project, correct the failure. You have the documentation to prove that you had another way that this project should have been handled. If by luck, the new manager used a similar method, you should have instant credibility in that manager's eyes. This could potentially help you get promoted in the future. (So you didn't overtly say I want your job, but through your actions and your manager's failures, documenting your goals might eventually help you get it).

- Suppose the manager uses your ideas, and the project is a massive success. Now you have documentation showing that this success was related to your plan. This could come up if you post for another position within the company. The new hiring manager might review your file and hopefully will see that you had a lot of ideas that led to great success. (I would also mention these things on the interview, then let him go back and verify it.)

GOALS - PERSONAL GOALS

For the company review process, we must know our audience when writing down our goals. We want to show the company that we are a valuable asset whose goals align with the company goals, we want to make sure we don't step on anyone's toes and make them feel insecure like you're gunning for their job (like a micro-managing boss). We want to make sure there is documented evidence of your ideas, so people can verify it in your personnel file (this is handy for both disciplinary and promotional situations). These goals are scripted for our target audience, they may not have anything to do with our real personal goals. Even though we will work on project X next year, assuming we are still working in the same department, project X is most likely not our personal goal. It may be a stepping stone we use to gain the experience we need to achieve our own goal (or maybe not). Our personal goals are goals that we keep to ourselves, the company may factor into the equation or perhaps not.

I like to perform a personal goal setting workshop once a year, but you can do it more often if you see a need (like your goals change in the middle of the year). I feel it's important to write everything down on paper, not a spreadsheet, physically write on pieces of paper. Some statistics prove that people who physically write down their goals are much more likely to achieve them. I use my personal goal setting workshop as a complete and total data dump of all of my goals, ideas, and the steps I need to take. It can get pretty messy when writing everything down and I want it that way, I definitely don't want to feel the constraints of cells in a spreadsheet or bullet points in a Word doc. While I'm working on my goals, I want to free flow, cross things out, write down too much info, whatever it takes. I do not want my mind to feel restricted in any way. So I use many sheets of paper to get my goals written down, then I memorialize my goals on a nice, neat spreadsheet afterward. This is how I recommend you perform your goal setting workshop each year.

WHY DO WE NEED TO GOAL SET EVERY YEAR?

There are several reasons that an annual goal-setting session is so valuable. First of all, goals tend to change over time. Goals that were once important might get superseded by a new purpose. Think about the guy who has a goal, since high school he's dreamt of buying a new Porsche. Since the day he graduated from college, he thought about walking into a Porsche dealer on his thirtieth birthday and purchasing a brand new 911 Carrera. Then his wife surprises him with a positive pregnancy test on his twenty-ninth birthday. He may choose to re-evaluate this goal with the latest information. Or maybe he decides not to change his goal. That is his prerogative. Or by goal setting, he might tweak his goal, so instead of a 911, he looks at one of the 4-door Porsche SUVs. Whichever the case, this is the power of goal setting and one reason I recommend doing it at least once a year, or if there is a significant, life-changing event that happens during the year, I'd take a cursory review of my goals at that point. (Think marriage, death, pregnancy, losing a job, getting promoted, winning the lottery.)

Another reason I like to set my goals at least once a year is because when I write something down, my mind reads it and then spends time trying to solve it. So if my goal was a little bit of a stretch, and what I mean by a stretch is at the present moment I have no idea how I am going to achieve this goal, my mind will continuously think about it. This may be subconsciously, but I believe the brain is always trying to solve problems, so by writing down your goals, you are unleashing your mind to try and solve for the unknown (In this case, how can I achieve this goal). Without getting all new-age, I think writing anything down will make you much more likely to remember, solve, and achieve it.

Did you ever get stuck when trying to solve a problem and decide to take a break? You document the process (or solution) that you've figured out so far. You go to lunch or leave for the night. Then an amazing thing happens. While you're eating lunch at Chipotle or you're in the shower the next morning, BAM, you figure out how to solve the problem. The solution just seems to materialize. I think, and I have no scientific evidence to prove it, but I think as you write something down and read it, your mind prioritizes it. And when there is no solution, your brain tries to solve the problem. And this happens behind the scenes, in your subconscious, so you don't even realize it's happening.

Ok, enough new-age bullshit.

When I think about my personal goals, I like to break them up into three buckets.

1. Goals I want to achieve this year (in the next 12 months)

2. Goals I want to start planning now to achieve within the next two to five years

3. Goals that will be achieved in five years or more.

Remember, there is no wrong or right goals, everyone's goals will be different. So don't skip writing something down because you're unsure of it, err on the side of writing it down because you are uncertain of it. Use separate sheets of paper (or a different tab in a spreadsheet) for each timeframe. So you'll have current goal sheets of paper, a mid-term goal sheets of paper, and the ten-year sheets of paper (or whatever your time frames are). Think about it like three separate goal-setting workshops. Goals from the first bucket can be a stepping stone to achieve something on the second bucket but plan for each separately.

When goal setting, I want you to think about the following acronym, it's a widely used method to set goals and objectives. It doesn't have to be perfect, but the more detailed you get with your goals, the more your brain will visualize them, and more importantly, visualize achieving them. Think of the following as the when, where, why, and how to accomplish the goals that you set.

BE SMART WHEN GOAL SETTING

Let's use a specific method for setting goals and objectives. Instead of just throwing a dart and seeing what we hit, let's follow a tried and true method for achieving our goals and objectives. This method uses the acronym S.M.A.R.T.

Your goals should be:

- **S**pecific

- **M**easurable

- **A**chievable

- **R**ealistic

- **T**imely

SPECIFIC

Be specific about what you want. Instead of saying, "I want to lose weight," be more specific like "I want to lose 20 pounds". But even that isn't specific enough, answer the what, where, when, and how questions. So, instead of just stating that you want to lose 20 pounds, you might say something like, "I want to lose 20 pounds by October 15th". Ok, so now you have the when but let's figure out the how, so let's adjust this goal to say, "I want to lose 20 pounds by October 15th, by bicycling three times a week, lifting weights two times a week, eat less processed foods and carbs, and I'll walk the dog every night after work". Ok, that is pretty specific, but it leaves out the most essential factor for you to actually achieve the goal. We often set the what, the when, the where, and the how. But the most crucial part of goal setting is to come up with an honest (and really specific) why.

We are much more likely to achieve a goal if we have an excellent reason as to why we must realize the goal. Heck, I'd even say we're much more likely to start a goal or resolution or whatever you want to call it if we have a good reason why. The reason needs to be very specific as well and will be different for every person. This might take a few hours of soul searching during your annual goal-setting session, where you sit quietly and really think about the reasons why you want to achieve the goals you've laid out.

Instead of only setting the very specific goal of "I want to lose 20 pounds by October 15th, by bicycling three times a week, lift weights two times a week, eat less processed foods and carbs, and I'll walk the dog every night after work" you'd add the why, "So I can get healthy and live a long and prosperous life. So I can have the energy to run around with my grandchildren and so I can be strong enough to play with my grandkids well into my eighties, and most importantly, so I can be alive to dance with my granddaughter at her wedding."

That is a very specific goal that covers, in detail, the what, when, how, and why.

MEASURABLE

The goal must be measurable. You need to be able to measure whether or not you are on track achieving your goal. Being very specific with your goals helps you measure them. If you had the goal "Be more successful next year" without explicitly defining what successful meant, then it would be tough to gauge whether or not you are achieving your goal. A better goal would be "to get a promotion next year" and then diving into all of the steps that you will take to get promoted. In that scenario, you could measure the actions taken and measure the actual result if or when you get promoted.

Let go back to our weight loss example. What can we measure to make sure we are on track to achieve our goal?

We can measure:

- How many times we rode our bicycle each week
- How many times we went to the gym each week
- What food we ate each week
- How many carbs we ate (or cut) in our diet
- Lastly, we can get on the scale and measure the results of the week

This helps us in a few ways. First, we can track our progress. Make sure we are performing the steps that we outlined during the goal-setting session. We are riding our bike three times a week. We are eating fewer carbs. Second, we can measure the effectiveness of our strategy. Is the diet and exercise program we set out to perform actually achieving our goal? Lastly, it allows us to adjust a little to compensate for any shortfalls in our plan. If we are halfway to our goal date and only lost eight out of twenty pounds, we need to rethink our strategy a bit. Do more exercise, re-evaluate our dietary choices, or both.

It's an old business adage **"If you can't measure it, you can't manage it"** by creating specific, measurable goals, we can manage the goals from the inception of the target until the day we achieve it. Always make sure you have a mechanism for measuring your goals

ACHIEVABLE

Ask yourself, is this goal achievable? Is this something that a human being can physically accomplish within the set timeframe? Now we've all heard of those competitive eating contests, where someone eats like 70 hot dogs in ten minutes, it might be achievable but probably not the best idea to set as a goal. (Unless your goal is to set a new competitive eating record.)

Let's go back to our 'lose 20 pounds' example. I'd think if you went to your doctor and weighed in at 200 pounds and your doctor tells you that your "normal body weight" should be around 150 pounds, then losing twenty pounds should be an achievable goal. (In fact, losing 50 pounds is an achievable goal). Conversely, if you were 90 pounds and your doctor tells you that your "normal body weight" should be around 110 pounds, then I don't think losing weight is achievable, at least not if you want to remain healthy.

The comedian Steven Wright was great at one-liners that really made you think. And he had a joke that went something like, "Anywhere is walking distance if you have the time." This summarizes this point perfectly unless stopped by an ocean or something like that, you can walk anywhere, say from New York and California. Assuming you can physically walk and are in good health, it is a possibility. But as we'll see in the next two steps of SMART goals, just because it is achievable, is it a realistic goal in the time allotted?

So, I view being achievable as something that is physically possible. Just because something is achievable doesn't always mean it's the best goal to set for you personally. So, before you even consider whether or not it's a worthy goal, make sure it is achievable.

REALISTIC

Just because something is achievable, doesn't mean it's realistic for you. As I mentioned before, I view something achievable as something that is physically possible. So, let's go back to our weight-loss example. We weigh 200 pounds and, according to our doctor, we need to get to 150 pounds to be at a healthy weight. We need to lose 50 pounds. Now, for anyone who ever watched My 600 Pound Life knows that it is very possible to lose 50 pounds within a year. It is physically possible, but is it realistic for you? When you only have 50 pounds to lose, can you stick to a rigorous controlled diet and exercise program that would drop about a pound a week from your waistline? There is no right or wrong answer. This 100% depends on you, what is realistic to you. Is losing 50 pounds within a year important enough to you, at this time? Can you stick to a strict 1,200 calorie a day diet and exercise regularly? I know myself; I'd probably be gung-ho the first month or two. But after I lost ten or fifteen pounds, I'd probably need to eat even less if I wanted to continue losing a pound a week, and I would probably need to exercise even harder as the weight started coming off. Now, you might be thinking, well, that would definitely motivate me to keep working out and dieting, "the more weight I lose, the more gung-ho I'd get," and you'd be right. Or you might be thinking, "Wait, I was doing fine eating 1,200 calories a day and exercising three times a week, but now I need to reduce my carbs, maintain 1,100 calories a day and work out four times a week, no way can I maintain this", and again you'd be right.

In case I just lost you, being realistic about a goal is a personal thing. Losing 50 pounds in a year is achievable and might be practical for some people but not for others. Knowing yourself, and being realistic, will go a long way in being successful with your goals. If you know you're the type of person that is gung-ho in the beginning and then your enthusiasm tapers off a bit, design your goal with this mind. Maybe lose 20 or 25 pounds in a year, you'll probably lose 15 in the first three months and can spend the rest of the year reinforcing the good habits you developed in the first quarter. So you may not lose as fast, but you are realistic about the goal, and you are setting yourself up for success by building healthy habits. If you lose more than 25 in the first year, then that's icing on the cake.

Maybe you are the type of person who sets a goal and sticks with it no matter what, you set the 50-pound weight loss for the year and design a plan for every week in the year. You schedule your calorie intake, your exercise routine, everything. If you don't hit the one-pound loss in a week, you'll double your efforts to make up the difference the following week. You remain entirely focused for the entire year, and you have no doubt that you will accomplish this goal.

This is the very essence of SMART goal setting. You were very specific, created a measurable goal, set an achievable goal, and are realistic when deciding whether or not you, personally, will achieve the goal. The last step, which we touched upon throughout the chapter, is timeliness.

TIMELINESS

You want to give your goals a timeframe. I like to bucket my goals:

1. Current bucket - one year
2. Mid-term bucket - two to five years
3. Long-term bucket - over five-year goals.

Every year I try and set up a few goals I'm going to achieve in one year (like writing this book, losing 20-50 pounds (depending on how gung-ho you are), save $1,000 in a savings account). I want to accomplish these goals within the year, so I usually only commit to two or three goals in the current bucket. If the goals are really short-term (achievable in less than a year), you can either modify the goal or set a new goal once you've achieved the first goal. For example, if your goal was to save 1,000 dollars in a savings account, and you're all gung-ho on New Year's Day to start saving, and by June you have the $1,000 savings fully funded. At this point, you could either increase the goal (say to $2,000) or create a totally different goal (start a new IRA, take a course to learn a new skill, or whatever you want).

- Two to five-year goals might be something like:
- Save 10,000 for a down payment on a new car
- Graduate college with a bachelor's degree in 'insert chosen major'
- Get a promotion or find a new company that has more growth potential
- Start a profitable business
- Take my significant other to that place they always wanted to go.

These are goals that you'll need to take steps to accomplish every month, but they won't be completed for two to five years.

Longer-term goals might be:

- Save a down payment and buy a house
- Become a (doctor, lawyer, CPA, tenured professor)
- Marry the person of my dreams
- Become the CEO of the company

- Have a business earning over a million dollars a year in profit
- Or the big one - retire, financially secure.

Like the two to five-year goals, these need to be reviewed and planned every year (starting right now). You don't want to wait until you're a couple of years out from retiring to begin to plan your retirement. (Start as early as possible, like right now!)

REVIEW YOUR GOALS, REGULARLY

Again, everyone's goals and aspirations will be different. This is why you should give yourself one afternoon a year, where you lock yourself up with no distractions and really set your goals for the year. These goals should be reviewed weekly (or at least monthly) throughout the year.

Schedule a weekly meeting with yourself to review your goals (literally throw some time on the calendar so nobody else can schedule a meeting with you during that time). When I consider my goals each week, I make sure I am taking some steps in the direction of achieving that goal. So, for our weight-loss example, I schedule the days I plan on exercising, maybe I'll prepare a new recipe to try for dinner one night. If it's a savings goal, I make sure I make some contribution to the savings account that week (or however often you get paid), or I'll eBay something and transfer the money into the savings. For longer-term goals (like going to college), I make sure I'm organized in my course work. I am actually scheduling the time needed for homework, to study, and to complete assignments. Every small step we take should help us accomplish the goal of graduating with our chosen degree.

I try to only have a few goals in the one-year (or current) bucket because we are also setting goals for the rest of our lives. Every goal we set, even goals that we won't accomplish this year, will still need us to take steps this year so we can achieve the goals in the future. For longer-term goals, you want to accomplish something every year towards achieving that goal. So if you need to save $40,000 as a down payment for a house and you want to purchase it in five years, just set up a savings account called House, and make regular contributions to that account for the next five years (It's only $154 a week (excluding interest), not so daunting after planning it five years ahead of time). If your goal is to become a CPA or a lawyer, make sure you schedule time with yourself regularly to study for the exam. Even though it will take a couple of years to get your license, there are things you need to do each week to succeed. You always want to be moving forward on your goals. You tackle significant goals one step at a time, that is how they get done.

I think following the SMART goal setting framework is a good starting point for setting goals in your life. Having specific, measurable goals that are achievable and realistic within a particular timeframe will increase your chances of accomplishing those goals immeasurably.

Goals should be set at least once a year but should be reviewed weekly throughout the year (or at the very least, monthly). This way, we are constantly reminded of the goal and the reason why we want (and why we need) to achieve the goal. This will make it much more likely that we accomplish it. You should set goals in all areas of your life, your health, your family, your occupation (or business). I always set goals for personal growth (whether it's to learn a new hobby or professional education, I think personal growth is one of the most important goals). I like to throw in something that makes me stretch (meaning it's out of my comfort zone, and I'll really have to discipline myself to accomplish it) - this year was writing this book. The stretch goal could be part of the personal growth goal or its own goal, but I think it's important always to try and grow a little each year.

Just have fun with it.

CHAPTER 12 - FREEDOM - OUR END GOAL

How can we do our work without having to worry about adding multiples or trying to look busy? Without getting new projects added to our job description? (without additional pay...) How can we manage ourselves, without being under the constant prying eyes of our manager? How can we do this while working in our pajamas if we want, without ever having to leave our home, no commute, no traffic, no added stress, and wasted time?

If you haven't guessed by now, the goal here is to work remotely. Most jobs only need a laptop and an internet connection to be able to do this. So you fly out to Hawaii on a Sunday work remotely Monday through Friday doing your normal nine-to-five. If your actual job resides on the east coast, you finish up at 12:00 PM Hawaiian time, and you can spend the rest of the day surfing. (Because of the time difference).

It sounds like a dream come true. For more and more people, this is actually becoming a reality. If you think about the idea of a call center, people are lined up, making phone calls the entire day. It really resembles the old factory worker mentality of the ninetieth century. If you worked at a factory in the late 1800s or during the 1900s, you had to be there physically. Because you were assembling parts or producing products (like car factories or textile mills) or something else physical (like printing newspapers). Even as a secretary, you had to be there and physically type on a typewriter. Nowadays, most jobs don't really need to follow this factory mentality, but, as we know, old habits die hard.

A company leases or purchases a large office to seat hundreds of people to staff a proper call center. The company must buy work areas, some sort of desk or cubicle, a phone, and a computer for each employee. Then it makes each employee commute to the office. Some are lucky and only need to commute ten minutes each way, while some have to take public transportation and transfer from train to bus, then walk a mile to get to the factory… I mean, call center. It seems a bit silly for a company to absorb all of the costs involved in setting up a massive call center. All people really need is a working phone line and the internet at home. A company can have a small call center in a small office where people work for the first few months while training, but once they know the position, then they can work remotely. This is true for a lot of jobs today. People used to have to go to the office/factory. They'd type up newspaper articles, work all night to meet deadlines, then the actual factory workers would have to print thousands of physical newspapers. Newspapers are still being printed. It's mainly for the older generations that sit every morning with their physical papers in hand. Reading while drinking their coffee (old habits die hard). Most younger generations just have a tablet or a laptop and read a few news sites to get caught up on the events of the day. So instead of having to come into an office, a news reporter just needs a computer and an internet connection to upload their article. The editor can see it and proof it (edit it) and then either publish it or kick it back to the reporter to update. You can have entire teams collaborating across the country or the world.

NOT THE DAMN MICRO-MANAGER, AGAIN

Another reason (you may have guessed) why it's sometimes so difficult to work remotely is because our manager is a raving micro-manager. If you do work for a micro-manager, it might be especially hard to be able to work remotely. As we know, micro-managers need to know everything you are doing, every minute of the day. So the idea of working remotely makes them feel like they are losing control. If they are insecure, they like to know that you are sitting ten feet away in case they need you to come into a meeting with them to explain things. They are comforted by the fact that you can prepare a presentation for them or some other technical stuff that they need your help accomplishing. Granted, you can easily make presentations remotely. But, with my experience working for micro-managers, they like to sit down and go over exactly how you came up with every single number (they need to "tick and tie" every number). I have found that this part, the actual explaining how I do something, usually takes twice as long as doing the actual work. We know that routines and control are critical to the micro-manager, so it may take a little more convincing for them to start to see the benefits to the organization. Sometimes it comes down to leaving the company to work remotely for someone else, and even that doesn't work 100% of the time. There is a good possibility that a dependent micro-manager would rather lose their right-hand man (or woman) then allow that person to work remotely. If you work for one of these types, you have to be a little more patient, possibly working it part-time. This way, they have time to acclimate the new way of life at the office and see that it's not really that big of a deal. But remember, old habits die hard.

LET'S TRY TO JOIN THE 21ST CENTURY

So how do we even start to get our micro-manager to warm up to the idea? Depending on your manager's level of dependency, this could be an easy sell or an absolutely impossible goal. I am going to outline a plan of attack to help you go from a cog in the factory wheel to becoming a remote Office Sleuth.

In the following steps I will outline your attack plan to get your manager on board with the concept of working remotely. If your company is stuck in the 60's, then there will still be a lot of red tape to cut, and we know if you work for a micro-manager that there is an entire mentality we need to change to even get the chance to work remotely. As you read the following, try and think as if you were in your manager's shoes. Think as if you are the company and someone is trying to sell the idea of working remotely to you. What I mean is you have to explain how the company will benefit from this new arrangement. So instead of saying something like, "I want to work from home so I can work in my pajamas, without having to commute to work in all that traffic and that you won't be able to look over my shoulder every five minutes...", you have to show the benefits for the company,

"Allowing me to work remotely will save the company $$$ a year and studies have shown (that we will talk about shortly) that workers are 13% more productive working from home, and I can be more flexible with hours according to the needs of the organization...". You get the idea. Every reason, every step you take towards working remotely has to benefit the company, somehow. Even though it's 100% for your benefit, it can never be about you, always the company. Use each of the following steps as part of an action plan to illustrate to your manager that working remotely would be the best solution for him (her) and the company.

You need to make sure to show how working remotely benefits the company. Studies have shown that employees working from home were 13.5% more productive. This study was conducted by a Chinese travel website CTrip. They gave employees the option of working remotely. They found that the employees that did work remotely made 13.5% more calls than the employees who worked in the office. (That is basically a whole extra days' worth of work every week for each remote employee.) After the trial-run at CTrip, some employees that initially chose to work remotely decided that they would rather work in the office (working remotely isn't for everyone). But the study found that the people who continued to work remotely (the people that really wanted to work remotely), their productivity went up even more significant than the original 13.5%. Working remotely allowed the employees to focus on work without being distracted by a bunch of meetings, meaningless chit chat with co-workers, traffic...etc.

Traffic is a real-time killer, even if you are on time to work, after a stressful commute sitting in traffic, it takes employees up to an hour to get their "heads in the game" at work. Stress from a commute lingers for a while, so it can take an employee a half to full hour to get 100% productive. Remote employees don't really have this problem.

Create an action plan. Go in armed with your idea, including all of the logistics to make this happen. Explain that you have really fast internet and a dedicated phone line. You have dedicated space in your home to work (take pictures of your home office). Explain that between the phone, email, instant message, Skype, conference call lines… it would be just like you were sitting in the office. Outline all of the work you do each week. Explain that the tasks can easily be done at home if there are things you need to actually come to the office to do, explain that you will come in for those weeks. (For example, if you have an annual audit, where auditors come to your office for a week, commit to coming into the office that week to work with the auditors). Don't be inflexible when asking for flexibility.

Ask for a one day a week trial and then kill it like a remote rock star. See if your manager will let you try working from home one day a week, if not call in sick one day but tell your manager that you have your laptop and that you are available. If your manager agrees to one day of remote work, you must make that the most productive day of your life. No multiples, no bull shit, just work your ass off. The theory here is that you've explained that studies have shown remote workers to be 13.5% more productive than their counterparts, now is your chance to prove it. The other thing you want your manager to realize is that the place really won't close down without you being there. You are accessible enough that your manager forgets that you are working remotely. You need to make it like you're ten feet away. So make sure you are reachable by phone, IM, email, whichever is your bosses preferred method to contact you. On this one-day trial run, you need to be ultra-responsive.

Know the current climate of the job market. As we mentioned earlier, knowing the current job market is a crucial piece of information to have. If you are in a recession and jobs are tough to come by (and even tougher to keep), you may not want to push the idea of working remotely too hard (at least until the job market turns around). Definitely bring up the advantages, see if they will give you a trial. Still, I wouldn't quit my job over it (in a recessionary job market). However, if the job market is hot, meaning there are a lot of jobs and only a few qualified applicants, then you have a little more leeway to push for a remote working arrangement. This is why it's so important to have your finger on the pulse of the job market. You need to know your industry. (Befriend a headhunter.)

Stress your worth to the manager, the team, and the organization. After you've had a good trial run, and you've proved that there's no real difference to the organization by working remotely (except for a little extra productivity), it's time to make the push for working remotely full-time. If you work for a neurotic, micro-manager, you may have to push hard for two days a week, then three... but keep pushing. Explain to your manager your worth to him (her) and the company. Reiterate all of the things you've spoken to him about during your annual review. Bring in the research you've done on current salaries in the job market. Especially if you are being paid less than the average, make a case for the salary range that people are being paid at other companies in your position. Maybe use your lower average salary to negotiate. Offer to remain at a lower wage as a remote employee. He might see this as a threat that you are (or you are about to) start looking for new opportunities. This is fine as long as you are a rock star and the job market is hot. Don't use this tactic in a recession. After showing your manager that your productivity actually increased and that you are easily accessible (where he forgets you are not in the office), make the case to work remotely. Agree to come into the office periodically for those monthly management meetings or during year-end or inventory, or whatever). Give a slight hint that there are a lot of great opportunities waiting for someone with your talent. This should get you at least a stable part-time remote working gig, even with the most micro-managing manager, at least three days a week. Always take it, then push for more. The more comfortable your manager becomes with the idea, the easier it will be to get to that elusive, full-time, remote working status.

An intriguing idea. That was what my manager told me when I offered to take a slight pay cut to work remotely. Now my situation was a little different because I was moving to another state, so it was either work remotely or find a new job. I thought it would be easier to get settled if I didn't have to start searching for a new job immediately, so I laid out a plan that I'd work remotely. What also made this a little different was that I literally told my manager I was moving and sprung the remote working situation on him all at once. I didn't work in any of the steps, over time. No trial run, no warning basically, I just offered to work remotely. So immediately, he shot down the idea (as I figured he would). He is a micro-manager and very dependent on me (I'm his right-hand), so the idea of me working across the country was initially not an option. After being denied that morning, I had to think of another option. I knew if this was going to work at all (even in the short term), I'd have to let it sink in, let him really think about it, and also give him an incentive to try it out.

So I drafted a 2-page proposal. I started by listing everything I did that could easily be accomplished remotely. First, with all of the ways we could communicate (phone, text, IM, email, screen shares, conferencing.) Then I listed every task I was responsible for accomplishing each month. 95% of them can be easily performed remotely. (Two audits would need my physical presence two weeks a year. I offered to travel back and work from the office for those weeks. And I also suggested that whenever he took a vacation, I would come in and cover the department for him.)

On the second page of the proposal, I made a complete game plan for the department (My action plan). I listed my plan for not re-hiring a recent termination, hiring a replacement for me in the office (a lower level but someone who can be present day-to-day), and best of all it would cost the company NO EXTRA MONEY because I offered to take a pay cut. This is why knowing the job market is so important. I knew the new job market where I was moving paid a little less than my current job paid. I was able to sweeten the deal with taking a pay cut.

I laid out the compensation arraignment and then summarized the whole deal in the last three paragraphs. I ended by saying, "let's try it out for three to six months." Basically, you have nothing to lose. I will put a copy of this proposal in Appendix II so that you can use it if you are ever in a similar situation.

How did it turn out? Well, I was hoping to get three to six months paid, working remotely as I settled into my new environment. At first, he was very intrigued by the proposal. Still, he needed to think about it and talk to the President and COO. (as I said, my boss is a micro-manager and a little insecure, he needs to hear other people's opinions to make a decision). I said 'ok,' and asked if he could give me a firm answer by Friday (it was Monday when I told him). Because if it's a no, I have to start sending out resumes and interviewing.

Friday came, and he said he talked to the President and COO, and they didn't think it was a good idea. It wasn't what I hoped for, but it didn't surprise me, so I started sending out resumes, making calls, networking. I gave him about a three-month notice, so he had plenty of time to find someone. About a month later, he sends me an email saying he started his search, and it will take him a little longer to find someone than he expected. He doesn't want to hire someone mediocre. Then he offers to keep me on during a "transition period" for at least a couple months or possibly longer. Now, this is kind of what I wanted the whole time, to be able to work remotely while getting settled into my new home. This allows me to remain employed, remotely, for a few months, training the new guy. My boss really doesn't understand the mechanics of what I do each month. He knows what needs to get done but not the actual steps to get it done. I will include his response in Appendix III so you can see that, while working remotely didn't work for me full-time. I ultimately got what I wanted. Now the ball was in my court because I could work remotely for a few months while looking for a new job. Still, if I found a new job, I could choose to continue to work remotely during off-hours to transition my replacement. It sounds weird, but it's a win-win.

CHAPTER 13 - CONCLUSION

Congratulations! You have officially graduated and have been promoted into the secret society of Office Sleuths. You have taken back control in the office from the insanity that can take place and have put some order back into your work-life-balance. Remember, you do not have to follow every single step in this book to make a drastically better work-life. (You never want to do something that will absolutely get you fired from a job, its always better to quit on good terms than get fired - think resume and references.)

Let's take a look back at what it means to be an Office Sleuth.

Think about your responsibilities

What were you hired to do? Each job assignment should have an allotted time frame (within reason), and then a multiple tacked on (for a little cushion). This cushion is what will keep you from having to finish everyone else's work because you are faster and more accurate than they are. It will prevent you from getting assigned busywork from your manager when he/she doesn't want to do it. Remember, there will always be more work to do. If you set yourself up as a superstar, someone who gets the job done in half the time it takes anyone else. You will become the "go-to" person to complete these little time-wasting assignments. Or the really huge, all-consuming projects that will eventually affect your actual work. I've been in that spot before, where I thought I was helping my career by assisting senior management with a project. I estimated the time it would take to do the project, but every time I thought I was done, the scope kept growing. Every day he was coming back to me to do another part of the project to where it started affecting my actual work. The senior manager figured that I offered to help, so they just kept using me to accomplish more and more of the project, which spiraled entirely out of control compared to the original assignment. I eventually had to explain the circumstance to my manager, (because it was affecting my work), and the two of them had to discuss. Finally, I was taken off the remainder of the project.

So what really happened? I thought I was advancing my career by helping a senior manager. It turns out that the project basically never ended. So when my manager spoke with the senior manager to get me off the assignment, I looked like I couldn't complete the project for the senior manager. Whether it was good or bad, I don't know, but he (the senior manager) never asked me to do another project for him. So instead of advancing my career, offering to help, it completely backfired and wasted about a week of my time. Plus, I didn't make an extra penny from doing all of this extra work. Remember the story of the kid raking leaves, and then the glass door broke. Don't volunteer to do extra work without making extra money, like a little overtime in your paycheck, or helping you get a better bonus or a possible promotion. Without any guarantee or even mention of one of these three things, don't jump into helping others just for the hell of it. What I've found over the years is what I think and what management thinks are usually two different things. So if they don't mention something you think you deserve, then they aren't thinking about giving it to you.

MANAGE THE LIST

You always want to keep a list of your upcoming responsibilities, this helps with the nagging email "It's a busy week, what are your deliverables this week?". The list really helps when your manager puts you on the spot, but it actually keeps you organized, helping you put each task in your schedule for the week. This also allows you to schedule your multiples each week. Some weeks might have a little larger multiple than other weeks, and there might be some weeks that you have virtually no multiples. This is usually a hell week when you have your regular responsibilities plus an audit and some other thing. Remember, you want to maintain your Rockstar status, so your boss trusts you. If they know they can depend on you during a very busy and stressful "hell week", they will be more likely to trust you when factoring in multiples during "normal working conditions."

The other thing you must keep is a list of all of the accomplishments you made during the year. I'd keep a weekly tab in Excel for all routine work and then a lead tab for all significant achievements. These are the ones you'll want to bring up during your self-evaluation and review. You can review the weekly task lists to see where you've taken on different responsibilities and also bring that up during the review. (E.g. - "Starting June 23rd, I took on the XYZ monthly project for customer X")

GO ABOVE AND BEYOND FOR YOUR MANAGER.

This is different than the example above, where you volunteered to do work for a senior manager that ended up absorbing all of your time for minimal benefit. This is always asking your boss if he needs help on projects that he probably doesn't want your help with, but he might occasionally agree and give you some extra work. Now, why would we do this? Simple. Your goal is to get your manager to TRUST you. If you offer to help him, and occasionally do some extra work for him, that builds trust. Once your manager is comfortable with you and starts to trust you, it makes your life as an Office Sleuth that much easier and much, much better. Remember, we are laying to the groundwork for a better work-life balance. A little extra work goes a long way in establishing trust, which goes a long way to create a better work-life balance.

GET TO KNOW YOUR MANAGER

The faster you learn who you are working for, the quicker you'll know how to deal with them, and the easier it will be to become a full-fledged Office Sleuth. Are you working for a micromanager? This is a critical question to ask and answer. The entire way you manage your workflow might stem from whether your boss is a micro-manager or not. Learn what your manager's capabilities and skills are. Are they technical? Do they understand what you do for the company? If not, you will have an easier time becoming a rock star than if they are super-technical and used to do your job before getting promoted. You can still become a very competent Office Sleuth, but you may have to make some changes to the way they were doing things for you to make the job your own. Your own Office-Sleuthy job…

ACE THE REVIEW

Take pride in your accomplishments when crafting your self-evaluation. This is the one time each year that you must pat yourself on the back and boast about your achievements. The most important thing to understand about the self-review is that it's your vehicle for getting a larger percent of the raise and bonus pool. (compared to your average, non-Office Sleuth counterparts.) You need to sell your boss on the idea that you should be promoted. (If that is what you want in this position). It's essential to keep up with the daily, weekly, and monthly lists to make the review process super easy. From the list, write about all of the accomplishments that you've made in the past year. Instead of just mentioning the things you've done, write them up in a way that shows how they were beneficial to the company and the department.

Write up the business goals that you'd like to achieve over the next year. This way, you are giving your boss a head's up in the way you think the annual review should go, and he/she can compare and contrast your goals with the goals that they want you to accomplish. (If your goal is to get promoted into a recently vacant position within the department, but your boss was considering promoting someone else, they can at least give some serious thought to promoting you before they go ahead and move someone into the role that you want. Maybe you don't get the promotion, but you want to make sure your boss knows you want it, and considers you, before moving ahead with another candidate. Who knows, maybe the other employee made no mention of wanting to be promoted on their self-review. You might get promoted just for writing up your desire and explaining why you'd be the best possible candidate for the job.) Remember, be SMART when working on your goals.

Be prepared for the face-to-face, annual review. Know the job market and your worth. Do as much homework as possible, so you are prepared to ask for what you are worth. Even if your manager comes back with a much lower raise than you thought, you will be armed to, at least, make your case why you deserve a larger percent than others in the department. (Or company, if your manager claims that it's a standard percent across the company.) The homework you do for the self-review and the annual review can net you the most amount of money (per hour) than probably anything else you do for the company. Remember, the difference between a 6% raise each year, and a 3% raise can translate into tens of thousands of dollars more in your pocket. (Could be hundreds of thousands over your entire career, depending on your position.) Even if you hate confronting your boss normally, this is the one time per year that you really need to force yourself to challenge your boss's assessment of you (your review). This is made a lot easier if you have done your homework. And come to the review armed with the facts. Your future bank account will thank you.

WORK REMOTELY

I think the ultimate way to work (and live) as an Office Sleuth is to be able to work remotely. Now we know that working for a micro-manager can make this much harder than it has to be. If you bring up the idea when you are talking to your boss, and he immediately scoffs, then you have some work to do. In the end, it will be worth it, but in the meantime, I wouldn't just bust into his office and tell him you are going to start working from home. You may not need to work remotely full-time to feel satisfied, so in the case of the dreaded micro-manager, try for a part-time stint at first.

If you live somewhere where it snows in winter, you can bring home your laptop the night before a storm and just tell him that you are working from home the next day. The key here is to bust your ass during this "trial run," your manager doesn't know it's a trial run. He just thinks it's storm related. You are setting a precedent. The key here is to work faster than you've ever worked before. As soon as he emails you to do something, response with an "I'm on it," get it done quickly, and email him back. (No, Multiples!). Respond immediately to any emails you get from people in the organization. You want the entire company to think that you're sitting at your desk in the office. There should be no discernible differences between working at home or in the office.

After your snow run, I'd periodically make up a reason to have to work from home. I have a guy coming to do something at my house, and I have to be home, so I'm bringing my laptop and work from home. You are getting your boss used to the idea. Over time, you can try for a regular one day a week. Use an excuse like, "My mother used to watch my son on Mondays but she…(the reason she can't do it anymore)". Make something up if you have to, I doubt he's going to go and check your mother's schedule. Now you work Monday's remotely. You can try and work in another day or two over time, use the same mother story, "Now she can't do Wednesday or Thursday either…". The key here is to make your boss feel as though you are sitting in your office. So to him, there is no difference whether you are on the company premises, working from home, or sitting in the coffee shop. Until your boss gets entirely onboard with the idea, you have to make some extra effort to be really responsive. The first time he needs you, and you're gone for more than a lunch hour, the micro-manager will probably pull the plug on the whole idea. I've seen it happen to a girl after giving birth. After her maternity leave ended, she worked out a two-day remote work schedule. I forget if she came in two days a week or worked from home two days a week. The first time my boss needed her for something, and she wasn't immediately available, he put the kibosh on her working remotely. The joy of working for a massive micro-manager!

Whether you're interested in working remotely or just having more freedom working in the office, being an Office Sleuth is the way to achieve that lifestyle. You will design a work-life that prevents you from getting wrapped up in other people's drama, stops you from taking on other people's workloads, and allows you to quit wasting your time working countless "overtime" hours for work that isn't even in your job description. I'm not saying don't help out and do what is necessary to achieve your goals. Whether it's to climb the corporate ladder or to be given total freedom to get your work done without interruption. I want that choice to be yours. Following the methods of an Office Sleuth or Office Rockstar (as I like to say) will help you achieve whatever goals you set for yourself. I'd love to hear about your Office Sleuth adventures. Visit officesleuth.com and send me a note. (While you are there, you can check out my ongoing cast of characters in my fiction stories about office life (based loosely on real people. It's a lot of fun.)

Until next time, Give Zero F*cks and Prosper!

GERARD HENRY

APPENDIX I

THINGS TO WATCH OUT FOR IN THE OFFICE

Do me a favor and just make the assumption that your office is monitoring every move you make. There is no privacy at your place of business. The company owns (or leases) everything; the building, the computers, the phone system, work cell phones, company credit cards, all physical files, and reports. Everything. Now know this. It is 100% within their rights to monitor any and all activities done on company hardware. And within the company premises (or even on their equipment outside of the premises). It's scary, big brother is definitely watching. You have no right to privacy at your employer's office or while using company hardware.

OK, do I have your attention?

The funny thing about this is that you most likely agreed to be monitored when you first started at the company. Remember that orientation you had, where you fill out a ton of paperwork, direct deposit, medical benefits, 401k, …etc. There was probably something called an employee manual or employee handbook that the company gave you to read. Then they had you sign a form saying that you read it and will adhere to the rules of the company (laid out in the handbook).

Most reputable companies will have an employee handbook for you to review and sign. Some smaller companies (or even some shady companies) don't make this information public knowledge. I will tell you that they still have every right to monitor you, so don't assume you're safe just because they never mentioned it to you.

I am going to lay out the top methods companies use to monitor their employees and some ideas to try to circumvent this spying.

PUNCHING IN

Punching in is probably the monitoring method in which we are most familiar. We've been conditioned to punch the clock from our very first "on the books" job back when we were teenagers. Nowadays, companies use a variety of methods to monitor employee's start and end times during the day. They've come a long way from the physical paper card that got punched in a time clock (which was really easy to circumvent if you have a friend working at the company). The most common methods companies use to punch in and out are either a biometric scanner or (for office workers) just have them employees use their computers.

Technically, exempt (salaried) employees shouldn't have to punch in and out. But a lot of companies will force this on all employees. They will give you a reason, something like, "We want to make sure all employees are at work" or "We want to make sure you're in the building." Trust me, only bad things will come from you punching in and out (for a salaried employee). You usually punch in when you arrive at work, punch out for lunch, punch back in after lunch, and then punch out before going home.

There are advantages to the hourly worker. They should get paid overtime if the clock shows them working overtime. But like every advantage, this can also become a disadvantage when your boss tells you that there is no overtime in the budget, and you need to punch out on time. Which seems ok until the day comes when you need an extra fifteen minutes to finish something. Then you need to ask permission. It can become a real pain. So, for the hourly worker, punching can be a good thing or not, it depends on the company.

For salaried employees, punching is never a good thing. Companies usually don't mention the time clock with their salaried employees unless there is a problem somewhere. If they want to write you up for some arbitrary reason, they can use the time clock against you. For example, say they want to fire you. Someone in senior management has a niece that just graduated from college, and they want to hire her for your job. With labor laws and discrimination cases running rampant, companies usually don't just fire people for absolutely no reason. Even if you are a complete f*ck-up. A good company will document the reasons why they are firing you. After trying to work with you, usually through a disciplinary action plan (traditionally called a PDP - performance development plan). To hire the niece, they start to look for a reason to let you go. Timesheets are an easy place to start. If you are late a couple times a week, then that is a great reason to start a PDP with you. It'll go something like this:

Boss: "I've noticed you were late three times last week and two times this week, so far. Attendance is crucial to us here at XYZ company. Consider this a verbal warning. You need to get to work on time." (And if he is a cowardly, micro-manager, he'll probably blame someone else. "The president of the company has tasked us with eliminating lateness, so my hands are tied, I have to write you up..." Don't let this fool you. It's his way of disciplining you without seeming like it's his decision.)

You: "Ok, I'll be on time from now on."

Two weeks later, a traffic jam from an accident, everyone (including the boss) is a little late...

Boss with HR representation: "You were late again today. I'm going to have to write you up."

And so on until they feel they have enough cause to fire you.

Conversely, what you never hear from your boss if you are a salaried employee.

Boss: "I see you have been working an average of 68 hours a week. I'm going to need you cut that back to 40."

There is no upside. You will never get accommodations for working too much. The only thing you might be able to do is to make the argument that being late two days for fifteen minutes is well offset by staying late for five hours. But, trust me, most companies that want to push discipline for lateness won't really care how late you work. I am not really a morning person. I like to get up early, but I'm not the type of person to arrive at work a half-hour before my job starts, I always put in extra time on the back end. Some people bring their breakfast and newspaper to work. Like an hour before work starts and they kick back and read the paper and slurp their Frosted Flakes. I was never that person. I always wanted to have a boss tell me that I need to make sure I arrive exactly on time every day, and then I can say something like, "Ok, I'll be sure to get here by 8:00 am every day, but then I'm leaving at exactly 5:00 pm every night." It's never happened, probably because they would lose five to ten hours a week on that trade, but it would be a fun conversation.

IT - MONITORING EMAILS, INTERNET AND CHAT (SKYPE)

Probably the most rampant spying that IT does on the employees of a company is done using electronic surveillance. No, I'm not talking about some high-tech spy games, I'm talking about your internet and email use on company property. Whether you work for a multi-billion-dollar company or a small start-up, assume everything you do on your computer is being monitored and recorded. Trust me, IT, and therefore, management has access to all of your emails.

How?

Some company's email servers will copy all email messages that go through them. Your boss will have a copy of every email you sent and every email you received. Creating a backup copy of all of your emails doesn't sound legal. But when we are using company property, they have the discretion to monitor all activity that happens on their machines (computers in this case). So just because you deleted emails doesn't mean they are gone for good. In fact, you may not be able to retrieve them, but your boss may be sitting on copies of them.

Another place where employees get in trouble is internet usage. This is definitely monitored almost everywhere they have internet access. A lot of companies will block sites they don't want their employees to go to. When you are on a company computer and type in a banned site, you will not be able to access that site.

Top types of banned sites at work:

Porn - for obvious reasons

Social Media - Facebook, YouTube, Twitter - being the time-sucks that they are

Online Shopping - Amazon, eBay - maybe the company wants to save you some money

Personal email accounts - Gmail, Yahoo Mail, Hotmail

Job search websites - some companies don't want to make it easy for their employees to look for another job

OPERATION: OFFICE SLEUTH

For every company, it will be different. Some companies might need you to access Facebook, while others ban it outright. Certain levels of employees may have access to websites, while other employees do not. Banned sites are usually the first step in monitoring your web usage (being that they don't need to track web usage on these sights).

Some companies will have a log of basically everything you do on your computer. Every program you open (including time stamps). Every website you visit and how long you spend on each site. It's a scary thought. Big brother is here. So you need to think it through whether or not it's really worth it surfing sites like Facebook at work. My thoughts are this. If there is any type of logical business reason to be on Facebook, then you can use that reason if ever questioned about why you've been on Facebook. (I do go to Facebook to research candidates coming in for interviews - a little recon - at least that is the story… ;-)

It's one thing to monitor sites you visit, but some companies take this up to a whole new level. They actually monitor your keystrokes. So not only does the company know you visited Facebook, but they know you left a comment on your friend's post. Or your chat with your boyfriend about your "plans tonight, assuming your asshole boss lets you leave on time." Or that angry email you started to type but then talked yourself off the ledge and never sent it. Your company now has it, even if you never sent it. This crosses over the line where privacy is no longer private. If you use a company computer to do anything personal at work, you have to assume your company can find out about it.

What can we do in this day and age to prevent the company from spying on your personal information? We all need to do that one personal thing during business hours. So how can we be sure that the company cannot record or monitor our private electronic communications and activities?

While at work, if you have to send a message on Facebook or make a quick stock trade, I recommend using your phone (and your phone's data plan - NOT COMPANY WI-FI) to do it. This way, the company has no record of the visit or the transaction. Remember, if you use your own phone and the company wi-fi, they can still see everything you did online. (At least every website that you visited), so use your mobile plans data at work to do personal tasks.

Are you working for a really paranoid employer?

Assuming that just knowing what, you typed (using the keylogger mentioned above) or logging what websites you visit for how long isn't even enough, companies can install software that will let them monitor your screen remotely. So not only will they know what you type, but they can see everything on your screen. Just search the web for "The Best Employee Monitoring Software" and see what names pop up. You can look in the task manager and see if you recognize any of these names in the processes. But I'm sure there are ways to hide these types of spying programs. I would imagine that would be a standard feature on employee monitoring programs. This is just something to be aware of. I doubt a company could monitor the screen activity for all employees eight hours a day. But keep your eyes and ears open, listen for any grumblings from other people. They probably would only spend the time and resources doing this if they suspected a problem. But I wanted to make you aware that this is possible (and legal) unfortunately. Remember using their property gives them the right to monitor the usage.

This call may be monitored for quality and training purposes…

Companies often monitor and record telephone conversations. This is done for legitimate (legal) business reasons. Suppose a vendor calls in and then files a complaint that an employee cursed him out on the phone. Having an actual recording would either prove he is telling the truth or lying. Without that recording, it would be his word vs. yours. Employers are allowed to monitor "business-related calls from their premises." But the problem is that when employers record all phone calls, your personal calls are also recorded. Even though an employer is supposed to tell you that they are monitoring personal calls, how is the monitoring system going to know which calls are private and which calls are business-related? I always assume that every call is getting recorded. Granted, a company should only pull up the recording if there is an issue. However, I still don't like the idea of a company having recordings of my private conversations. So we go back to the golden rule, "If you are using company equipment, they can monitor what you are doing with that equipment."

Again, I go back to using your personal cell phone to make personal calls. Even if a company issues me a cell phone, I always keep my own phone with me at all times. I know that it's so obvious that you are on a personal call when you use your cell phone in the office. I'd rather take five minutes to have a quick personal call on my cell phone and not be recorded than possibly get recorded.

Besides phone tapping, your company can also access your voicemails. This is a good reason to monitor your voice mails regularly (and to tell your friends not to leave personal messages on your company voicemail). Your friends should have your cell phone number. Besides personal voice messages, if you don't listen to business voicemails within a certain period, and the company does monitor it, you can be held accountable for not following-up on a potentially time-sensitive voicemail. Just something to think about.

What if your employer has cameras set up all over the office, is this legal? Of course. You are on their premises and they can record if they want. Now I haven't seen too many office buildings set up actual cameras throughout the office. I think that would make for a massively paranoid workforce, but can it be done, is it being done? Absolutely. I'm not talking about a store or a bar where cameras are pointing at the registers. I'm talking about being videotaped in a cubicle while you are working. That would be creepy. I doubt I would stay at a job that recorded me like that, but every circumstance is different.

Areas that companies might record audio or video are meetings, reviews, and disciplinary actions. They should tell everyone that they are being recorded but who knows, every company is different. I think it's a rare exception to be recorded like this without being told, but it does happen. On the flip side, there is a good chance the employee is recording the conversation if they know they are being disciplined. So, if the employer says something discriminatory, the employee has it recorded. (This is why smart employers will give verbal and written warnings, and gradually escalate the disciplinary procedure. So, there is enough cause for termination.) I wouldn't worry too much about being audio or videotaped. Unless you see the cameras. Or hear about someone who was presented with a recording of their actions during a review. I just wanted to mention that this is a possibility.

PEEPING TOM

Have you ever worked somewhere, and there is always this weird feeling of prying eyes? I worked at this company where the owner would casually hang out by the door of my office. And then, ever so casually, would lean over and peek into my office to see what I was doing. It was bizarre. My boss was peering into the office on the sly and trying to catch me doing something. And it's funny if I'm working my ass off getting things done, he's not going to say, "Hey great job, thanks," but if I check the stock market the moment, he begins his stakeout, I'll never hear the end of it.

A lot of people think because their computers are facing the back wall that they are safe, but you have to look at your surroundings. If you have windows behind your desk and it is dark outside, then everything on your computer monitor is now visible in the window. I always pull my shades all the way down to eliminate those "prying eyes." If you don't have shades, then keep a bunch of programs open so your screen is covered with different windows. Oh, and always have a good excuse, at the ready, for why you are on a site. If your boss sees you online, you initiate the conversation, "Apple missed earning today, holy shit…". I worked with one guy who had filing cabinets behind his desk, so when he was working in the filing cabinets, he was turned completely around. So, he hung a mirror up on the back wall, so when he was facing backward, he could see what was going on behind him. I'm not saying you need to get that paranoid, but I had to share that story.

SWIPE IN / SWIPE OUT

Do you work at a company that makes you use a badge (or some kind of card) to swipe in when you arrive at work? Maybe there are certain areas of the building you need to use that badge to enter. Like one company I worked had the C-Suite (executive wing) only accessible by swiping in and out with the badge. This tracks two things. This monitors your location during the day, and also how long you were in a particular area (assuming you need to swipe out as well). Like the timecard (or time clock), this also monitors lateness and extended lunches. An example I can use is suppose your company has a reception area, where people are free to walk into during the day. But to get into the building, you need to swipe in, using your access card (or badge). So the company can pinpoint the exact minute you arrive at the office. Now you go to lunch and need to swipe out (I'm not sure if this is a fire hazard but bear with me). So, the company will have your exact times in and out every day when you arrive and leave for work and your swipes out and then back in for lunch. Granted, it makes total sense from a security standpoint, visitors are usually given a temporary visitor badge. This also makes sense for the company to restrict access to certain areas. From the employees who shouldn't be in that area without an invitation. So, you are benefiting from added security, but just know this is just another way you can be tracked.

REMOTE ACCESS

If you are one of the fortunate ones that work remotely and think you are entirely safe from the company's prying eyes, not so fast. Companies can implement remote tracking software that tracks your productivity. These types of software vary in the amount of "big brother-ness" with some allowing for remote screen captures during the working day and others monitor your activity. This is probably more prevalent with a company that employs a large number of remote employees, but just be aware. This software also can track your location, which is good and bad. Bad if you are supposed to be in Pennsylvania, and you are working in the Bahamas, but useful if you are in Pennsylvania, but your laptop is visiting the Bahamas. A lot of these programs can not only pinpoint your location for law enforcement (in the event of theft) but fortunately can also wipe the hard drive remotely (in the event of a theft).

LO-JACK

If you are a remote employee that drives a company vehicle, there is a good chance the company has installed GPS tracking on that vehicle. This can help if the vehicle gets stolen, but it tracks every move you make during the day. Just understand the company will get a report showing exactly where you went every day and how long you spend at each location. This shouldn't be a massive surprise, but I want you to be aware that this is probably happening on your company vehicle.

There are some good reasons to track a vehicle using GPS:

- To improve response time
- To enhance the efficiency of routes.
- Accurate timekeeping records.
- Increasing safety and productivity
- Like we mentioned above, helping recover a vehicle after a theft.

But some employers monitor employees all the time (even during non-business hours). This becomes a problem when your employer gets a report that you were speeding because you had to race to pick up your child who needed to be rushed to the doctor. The company only sees the speeding but doesn't know the reasons behind it, so technically, you can get in trouble from the company for personal driving you do after working hours.

Also, an employer can monitor remote employees through the GPS on their mobile phones. Just be aware of this when a company issues you a phone. There is a good chance that they can monitor the activities done on that phone, including location tracking via GPS.

MONITORING YOUR PERSONAL FILES/DIRECTORIES

The last area I want to talk to you about is personal directories. Some companies have a directory with your name on a different drive that only you can access (well, that's what they tell you). If your company's network directory lies on the J drive, maybe your personal directory resides on the P drive. Every employee is allotted a certain amount of space on their personal drive. (You can usually get more space if needed, but if your position shouldn't have a ton of personal information, this may be a red flag for IT. Just remember that IT giveth and can taketh away, and definitely can see anything in that directory.

Now, the best way to circumvent the prying IT eyes is to make a folder with your personal info and password protect the folder. (There are different ways to do this. Depending on which operating system you are working. You can do a quick search online "How do I password protect a folder in x (x = os version)." This will require you (or anyone) to enter a password every time you access that folder. Again, if IT or management find this, then it becomes a huge red flag unless you deal with sensitive information (like payroll).

If you must access personal files at work and do not want to save anything on a company directory, the best thing to do is create a free Dropbox (or some other file storage service) account. I usually use my work email address for this account. This will give you a couple gigabytes of storage for free. Now you can sign in and save and retrieve any file you want. (Just make sure you aren't eating so much bandwidth that IT sends that weird email asking if they can hop on your machine and take a look...)

I wouldn't save massive multimedia files on your company drives (better just to access YouTube or a similar service). Things like your resume, personal data, private lists (like if your moving and have a bunch of info on a to-do list, and you don't want prying eyes to see). These are perfect for either a password protected folder or a Dropbox. Remember the golden rule. Anytime you are using company property, they are most likely spying on you (or at least they definitely can, both legally and technologically).

Now that I have you really, really paranoid, I'll mention that most companies probably aren't doing all of these things. They either don't see a need or just don't have the IT resources to spend the time monitoring everything. What they are doing is most likely all laid out in the employee handbook - I suggest you re-read it, remember you signed it...

To all my Office Sleuths: Be careful and have fun!

APPENDIX II

THE PROPOSAL (ACTUAL)

I've given this some thought and would like to make a proposal, where I think you can keep me on board without really costing the company any money.

With all the tools at our disposal, working remotely has become much less of an issue.

- Phone
- Text
- IM
- Email
- Screen shares
- Unlimited conferencing
- Teleconferencing (Skype)

Things I can do remotely:

- Margin analysis
- Budgets/forecasts (F,P&A)
- Analytical work
- Senior management meeting

- PowerPoint presentation
- Physical presentation (Teleconference into the meeting)
- Month-end close review and work
- Commissions
- Accruals
- Monthly reporting (book)
- Board book
- Tax filings and review
- ACH payment approvals
- Department meetings
- Manage our credit card account, Amex, Visa, Concur
- Banking – wires, borrowing base…etc.
- AP Check runs (just need someone to get checks)
- Any ad-hoc analysis that you need
- Things I can travel back to the office:
- Come to the office for Audits (financial & bank exam)
- Come in to cover your vacations.

Proposal:

Granted, with working remotely I'll lose a certain aspect of the day to day activity in the office. However, I can still be a very valuable part of the team, even working remotely. I have a solution that would allow me to work remotely while keeping the department intact without costing the company any money.

The first thing is reducing our headcount by one, the X position. Between XX and YY overseeing the day to day and I can take care of all the other responsibilities remotely, we wouldn't need that new hire.

Secondly, my replacement. I will still be in the loop with daily communication, but you'll probably want a manager level employee to oversee the day to day operations. I'd recommend hiring an accounting manager to replace me in this capacity.

I love working for this company. I'd like to stay on board in some capacity. All the things that I outlined above can be done whether I'm sitting in the office or in my home office. Plus, I hate interviewing (smiley face)

<u>Here is my proposal.</u>

Sometime in February, I will move to New place.

When I move, I will take a pay cut down to $XXX,XXX (no bonus, except at the discretion of the company)

We won't re-hire Position X so that will save us $XXk

We hire an accounting manager for $XX-XXXk (Saving about $XXk from my total compensation)

Eliminating X and hiring an accounting manager at $XXk will save you the $XXXk. I will remain on board to take care of all the items above. I'll handle any special projects, train the accounting manager, and someone to lean on when you need me to come into the office. (Audits, vacations... etc.)

I'd be available via, phone, IM, conference call, text, we can share screens or use the laptop camera to be visible in meetings. It'll be like I'm sitting in my office.

I think this would work. **For no extra money, we're trading in a staff position for me working remotely.** As I mentioned earlier, I love working here and don't want to leave. I realize the move would put some strain on the day to day operations, but I think a good manager would be able to handle it. **At the very least, we could try it out for 3 - 6 months and re-evaluate.** If it's not working for you, then we'll have a conversation at that point.

Please let me know what you think.

APPENDIX III

THE DELAYED RESPONSE

I've been thinking about the transition after you move to {New Place}. Right now, The Recruiter has started the search for your replacement. I have a feeling it might take a while. I'm certainly not settling for a mediocre candidate. Once we do land on someone, I would like to have a solid training/transition plan in place. I know you're scheduled to move the end of Feb/early March. I'd like to be able to commit to keeping you on for at least through April 30, but we need to figure out how a transition plan will work logistically. Think about it and let me know. **If I can guarantee keeping you on through April (possibly longer), it gives you ample time to settle in without the added burden of finding employment right away.** I would just need you to help me with the transition/training.

www.ingramcontent.com/pod-product-compliance
Lightning Source LLC
Chambersburg PA
CBHW070625220526
45466CB00001B/96